I0036184

Colophon
Authors: Gijs van Bilsen, Joost Kadijk, Cyriel Kortleven
With: Patrick Short
Design: Esther Vorstenbosch
Translation: Philip Chimento

ISBN: 978-90-819506-1-9

The authors have tried to retrieve the rightful owners and inventors of the exercises
mentioned in the book. If you feel that your work is not mentioned in the rightful way,
please contact the authors. This work is licensed under the Creative Commons Attribution-
NonCommercial-ShareAlike 3.0 Unported License. That means that you are free to:
to Share — to copy, distribute and transmit the work
to Remix — to adapt the work

Under the following conditions:
Attribution — You must attribute the work in the manner specified by the author or licensor
(but not in any way that suggests that they endorse you or your use of the work).
Noncommercial — You may not use this work for commercial purposes.
Share Alike — If you alter, transform, or build upon this work, you may distribute the resulting
work only under the same or similar license to this one.

To view a copy of this license, visit http://creativecommons.org/licenses/by-nc-sa/3.0/ or
send a letter to Creative Commons, 444 Castro Street, Suite 900, Mountain View, California,
94041, USA.

FORE-WORD

Yes And...Your Customer Service

The added value of improvisation in organizations

Authors

Gijs van Bilsen

Joost Kadijk

Cyriel Kortleven

With a special chapter by Patrick Short

3

A book about improvisation. How absurd. Although I totally agree
with the power of using improvisation in your professional life,
I also believe people should practice what they preach. And writing
a book, with the long process of editing, re-reading, and more editing,
is everything but improvisation. However, I understand that it is a
necessary evil. In order to spread the advantages of improvisation,
one should use all forms of media.

Knowing the authors as I do, I know that they used all the rules of
improvisation in the book. They 'yes, anded' each other's suggestions
while reviewing the drafts; they stayed in the moment, even locking
themselves up without Internet access while writing; they made others
look good by putting in their colleagues' favorite exercises; and they
dared to fail, especially in meeting deadlines.

So, maybe, improvisation and writing a book do go together.
If that is possible, it should also be possible to read a book and
improvise at the same time. To that end, I would advise you to treat
this book as a workbook. Since improvisation is thinking and doing
at the same time, you should do the things written here. Even the
theoretical part lends itself to experimenting with improvisation
in all different ways. Try putting the book down after you read
something interesting, and putting it into practice.

Let me close with the words that it is my belief that using improvisation, as this book teaches it, will make the world a better place.
This may just be the rambling of an old man, but I hope you'll see
why I believe this after reading the book.

Enjoy!

Prof. Oegnar Wedendorff

EXTRA FOREWORD TO THE SPECIAL EDITION

Gijs, Joost and Cyriel have written a book that truly explains improvisation as a system, or series of systems.

We learn how to apply improvisation to personal and organizational systems, both applied and in performance.

We learn the Seven Habits of Effective Improvisors.

We learn about Leadership and Creativity through the lens of improvisation.

We learn about Multicultural Organizations and how embracing different approaches makes us stronger.

Since 1989, I've been working with corporate clients to help them bring an improvisational perspective to their work. As you might expect, the early years of this effort were focused on sales, marketing, management and design areas; this was driven by customer demand.

In the past decade, there has been an acceleration of demand from customer service areas of client companies, and it's getting to be a larger and larger percentage of my work. Managers and owners are realizing that something critical is missing when we try to systemize every contact with our customers. Customers have different stories. We need to hear them. We need to accept them.

We are beginning to understand that each customer is unique. Serving those customers is not a cost or a problem, but an opportunity.

Improvisation brings us a set of skills and tools to take advantage of this new outlook.

It's a privilege to join Gijs, Joost and Cyriel with a chapter that applies improvisation to customer service. I hope that you take at least some of it to heart. If we serve with our hearts, good things will happen.

Patrick Short
CSz Portland (Oregon, USA)
September 2014

TABLE OF CONTENTS

With an additional chapter by Patrick Short

Introduction

In this book we combine improvisation and creativity with organizational development. Throughout the years we have worked as trainers, coaches and organizational consultants. We have discovered the power of improvisation as a skill for helping professionals and managers cope with the increasing complexity of their work and the increasing speed of change. Change is happening faster and faster, the professional needs to be more flexible and thus needs to improvise more.

This book is for managers, trainers, coaches, and professionals who want to increase their improvisational skills for better results. We are convinced that improvisational skills make better professionals and managers, better teams, and ultimately better organizations. In this book, we will explore the benefits of improvisation on a professional and organizational level.

This book is created through teamwork. The three authors have each written their own part in their own style. Besides that we have asked colleagues all over the world to contribute to this book with their favourite exercise, story or insight.

Organizational improvisation is a new domain in organizational development. The development of knowledge is growing day by day through the professionals that are working with their clients.
If you want to stay up-to-date please visit our website:
www.yesandyourbusiness.com for the latest news, articles, updates and discussions.

THE FRAME-WORK

CHAPTER 1

PART I

IMPOR-
TANCE OF
IMPROVI-
SATION

Part 1 consists of a general introduction to improvisation: what is improvisation and what are its uses? We will give an overview of the book by presenting four different sides of improvisation, and conclude with a chapter on how to deal with improvisation in an organizational context.

In this chapter we describe the different sides of improvisation in order to frame improvisation in an organizational context. At the end of this chapter we introduce the rest of the book.

1.1 THE DIFFERENT SIDES OF IMPROVISATION

Improvisation is a catch-all term which we aim to define more accurately in this chapter. Improvisation is multifaceted and it is this versatility of improvisation which we like to discuss in greater detail, to show that it is much more than an art form in jazz or theater.

Definitions
What do we mean when we talk about improvisation?

Improvisation:
- a performance which an actor, musician, etc. has not practiced or planned
    - *a blues/jazz improvisation*
    - *There are classes in movement, dance and improvisation.*
- when you make or do something with whatever is available at the time
    - *I'm afraid we don't have all the necessary equipment, so a little improvisation might be required.*

(Definition of *improvisation* (noun) from the Cambridge Advanced Learner's Dictionary & Thesaurus © Cambridge University Press)

Improvisation is the practice of acting, singing, talking and reacting, of making and creating, in the moment and in response to the stimulus of one's immediate environment and inner feelings. This can result in the invention of new thought patterns, new practices, new structures or symbols, and/or new ways to act.
(Source: wikipedia.org; search term: Improvisation)

The essence of both definitions is that improvisation is unprepared and spontaneous, using the resources at hand. In addition, both definitions are linked to art forms like theater and music. In this book, we call improvisation as an art form by its colloquial name 'improv' and all other forms will be referred to simply as 'improvisation.'

Improvisation follows rules and principles

Improvisation as a skill, like driving a car or learning a language. Some people may be more talented than others, but like any other skill, it needs practice, rather than talent.

Jazz musicians and improv actors on the stage hone their skills in being spontaneous and improvising. By playing and rehearsing together a lot and by observing a few basic rules, it is possible to learn how to improvise and how to play off each other. The basic rules ensure that improvisation does not turn into chaos. Musicians, for instance, will agree on a key, a time signature, and a basic chord pattern. Within these parameters, they have the freedom to improvise and play variations on the basic chords.

Improv actors also have a set of basic principles. We will explore this in the next section.

1.2 WHAT IS IMPROV?

Improv, improvisational theater, is based on the principle that people are at their most interesting when they act in the here and now, when they are in touch with themselves and their surroundings, when they accept and respond to both internal and external impulses.

The founder of improv is Keith Johnstone. He developed it as a counterpart to plays with rehearsed parts and characters, with the purpose of reintroducing a sense of fun into acting. It is sometimes also referred to as 'theater out of nothing.' Improv became known as a result of a performance form called Theatresports. Introduced in 1988, this became a popular form of theater in no time. In this version, two groups of actors make up scenes based on suggestions from the audience. Later on, different TV shows appeared that were based on Theatresports.

Improv operates on a number of basic principles:
- The stage is safe.
- There is no such thing as making a mistake.
- Everything is possible.
- Don't tell, just act.
- Silence your inner censor.
- Abandon your own plan.
- Expand and use your powers of association.
- Accept other people's ideas and build on them.
- Work together and make sure your fellow actor is having a good time.
- Use the other person's impulses for a scene.
- Don't hesitate, just do it.
- Trust yourself and the other person.
- Seek out risk and court danger.

The majority of these basic principles are largely similar to those of the creative process (see chapter 4.) Here, too, you need to expand your powers of association, postpone your judgment, accept and build on other people's ideas. Improvisers are creative people who can come up with new ideas on the spot and bring these ideas to life.

The principles don't only apply to the stage, but to everyday life as well. We'll visit the '7 Habits of Great Improvisers' in part 2, Professional Skills.

A WORK-SHOP BY KEITH JOHNSTONE

I want this to be a safe place.

The founder of improvisational theatre, the Englishman Keith Johnstone, lives in Canada these days and regularly gives workshops all over the world. Attending one of these workshops is a really special experience. I, Joost, had the pleasure of doing so one weekend back in 2006. Johnstone is best described as a big, mischievous child, with an unbridled imagination and boundless energy. He is a born storyteller who inspires people to produce wonderful per-formances and he has a very sharp eye.

Every session begins in the same way. Johnstone sits flopped out on a sofa and waits for the participants to sit down around him in a circle (at a suitable distance) with a nervous sense of anticipation. Johnstone gives everyone a friendly nod, waits until things have gone quiet and then goes on to do the following: he extends both hands in front of him, makes a wide gesture, encompassing the stage before him, while saying the words: I want this to be a safe place. This one-sentence expression embodies the most important basic principle of improv, which is safety. The actor has to feel safe on stage, safe enough to do anything that comes up in his mind at that particular moment, without feeling that his fellow actors are giving him funny looks or judging him for it.

1.3 THE FOUR DIMENSIONS
OF IMPROVISATION

Improvisation is often associated with theater and music. We call this the creative or artistic side of improvisation. A wonderful example of the theatrical side of improv is Whose Line is it Anyway, a British TV program. It was hugely popular in the nineties and its format has been copied in many countries. In the USA, big stars like Whoopi Goldberg and Robin Williams made guest appearances on the program, which contributed to its high ratings and huge success. The premise of the program is that a number of trained improv actors act out several standalone scenes with input from the show's host.

Another example we are no doubt familiar with is jazz improv. For instance, Miles Davis' CD "Kind of Blue" is a landmark in the genre.

But there are other dimensions to improvisation apart from the theatrical or musical ones. We have already established that the quality of being 'spontaneous' and 'unprepared' gives us the ability to improvise. This ability to improvise is expressed in four different ways:

1. Improvisation as a collective and free art form
2. Improvisation as a means to support individual development
3. Improvisation as a professional skill
4. Improvisation as part of a collective behavior and organizational culture

Let's take a closer look at these four ways of expression:

1. Improvisation as a collective and free art form
   In this form, groups improvise together to create beautiful things. The typical thing about this form of improvisation is that it is a collective form of expression and the aim is to produce something beautiful, to contribute to a collective work of art. This can be on stage but can also be a collective painting or

sculpture. The collective creation process is governed by a few rules. This form draws quite heavily on people's artistic creativity.

2. Improvisation as a means to support individual development
   In this form, improvisation is primarily used to stimulate individual and personal development. Improvisation is used to clear the mind and get 'into the now,' to become aware of personal characteristics and blocks, and to grow as an individual. In this form, improvisation is used as a coaching tool, an instrument of meditation, as part of drama therapy or as a way to express feelings and emotions and consequently grow closer to yourself.

3. Improvisation as a professional skill
   In this form, improvisation is used as a supporting tool in skills training courses. Improvisation appears in different guises as a means to train communication, creativity, negotiating, teamwork, and management skills. Training your improvisation skills and improving your ability to improvise will help you grow as a professional and as a manager. Many instructors use improvisation exercises in their coaching sessions. A colleague once said of improvisation that it is an 'all-in-one soft skills' training course. The exercises in this book aimed at developing creative skills can also be used in this way in training courses. More and more coaching agencies are discovering and harnessing the power of improvisation.

4. Improvisation as part of a collective behavior and organizational culture
   In the fourth form, improvisation has become part of the rules of an organization. Here, improvisation is no longer a skill to be developed separately, but it has become embedded in the DNA of an organization and has become part of the organizational culture. This type of organization has as little hierarchy as possible and a preference for a flat organizational structure. Often, there is only a basic set of rules which govern the behavior of the organization's members. The rules have become the code of conduct for the organization's culture. The result is a flexible organization which allows its professionals a lot of responsibility.

21

We find elements of an improvisational culture in organizations such as Google, 3M, Gore and Pixar Animation Studios. At 21 Lobsterstreet, the company of Joost Kadijk and Cyriel Kortleven, we have also built on a simple set of ground rules, and a simple and minimal organizational structure.

The improvisation matrix

When we take a closer look at the four forms of expression of improvisation, we can see that they can be organized into a framework with four quadrants and along two axes, the improvisation matrix:

1. individual-collective (horizontal axis)
2. personal-organizational (vertical axis)

On the horizontal axis, we see improvisation as a means to support individual or collective development. Improvisation can help give you greater insight into your own psyche as an individual, or become a better professional.
On the opposite side of the axis, improvisation can be seen as a means to serve the collective. It helps the collective create more beautiful things or function better as a group.

On the vertical axis, we can see improvisation as a means to support organizations and the professionals working in them, and to improve organizations' performance. Improvisation supports the development of the professional within the organization.
At the top of the axis is the person on their own. Improvisation is used here as a means of expression to create art or to support the exploration of personal qualities.

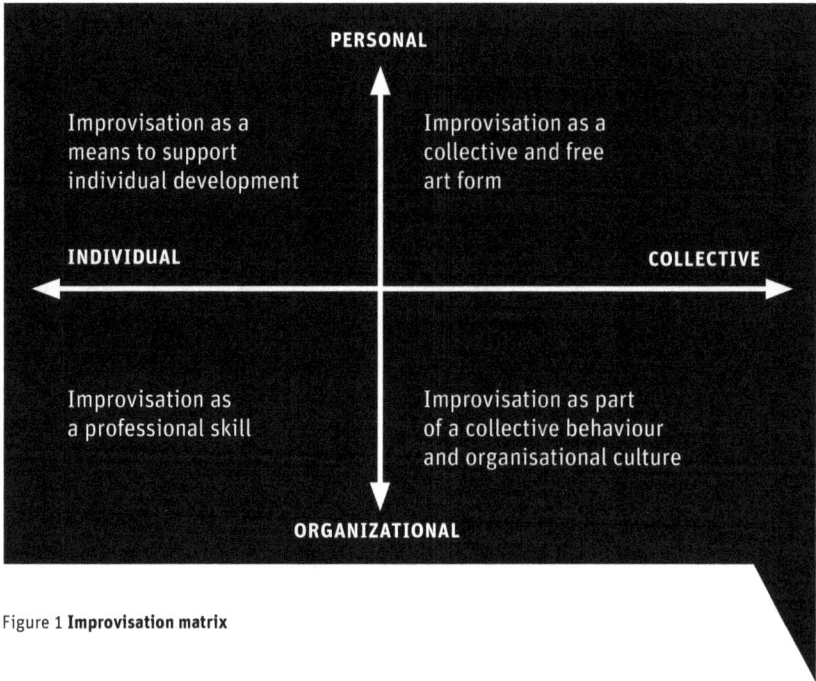

Figure 1 **Improvisation matrix**

1.4 FOCUS OF THIS BOOK

This book focuses on the lower half of the improvisation matrix. The theory and the exercises help to develop professional skills, and support team building and organizational development. We have divided the book into an introductory part about improvisation in organizations, a second, theoretical part about professional skills, and a third, practical part with exercises. In the first two parts we will look into the following topics:

- The background of improv theater and the basic rules of improvisation.
- Organizational improvisation. We explore the benefits of improvisation in organizations and apply it to themes like organizational structure and leadership. We support this with recent management literature on the use and function of improvisation in an organizational context.

The third part of the book is the toolbox. In this toolbox we describe more than seventy exercises that will help you put the theory into practice. We have tested all the exercises ourselves. On top of that, we have asked top improvisational trainers around the world to share their favorite exercises with us.

The exercises are written down in the form of instructions. Many of them can be used even by inexperienced coaches. Some of the exercises are videotaped and have been placed on our website www.yesandyourbusiness.com.

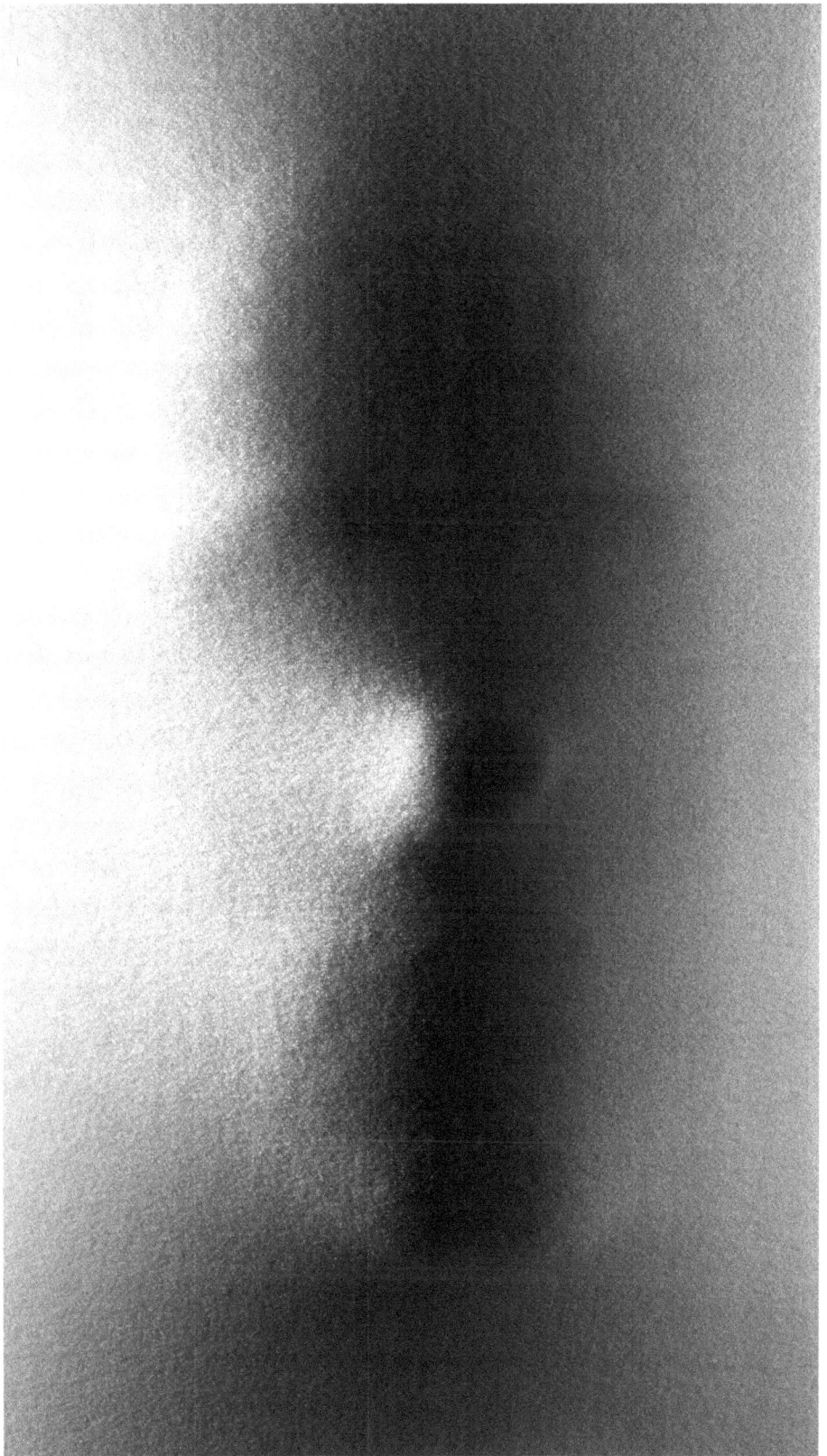

ORGANI-ZATIONAL IMPROVI-SATION

CHAPTER 2

In this chapter, we will take a closer look at the increasing complexity, turbulence and time pressure in our society,
how organizations respond to this and how organizations
can use improvisation not only to cope with, but to take
advantage of these forces[1].

[1]Unless otherwise noted, most of the information in this chapter and the next is taken from a
scientific literature review by Gijs van Bilsen. The original, with references to all of the sources,
is available at www.organizationalimprovisation.com.

2.1 INCREASING COMPLEXITY

Improvisation as an art form, the upper right quadrant of figure 1, is well established in both jazz and theater. Improvisation as part of collective, organizational behavior and organizational culture is becoming ever more important. This is because the world is becoming ever more complex.

Our brains are constantly bombarded with ever more and ever faster impulses and also have to process an increasing amount of information. What's more, they have to make increasingly snap assessments and decisions based on this information.

Within organizations, the flow of information is getting bigger all the time, with a massive 200 billion (200,000,000,000) e-mails being sent on a daily basis globally. According to Socialnomics. net, the average e-mailuser receives 507 e-mails per day. This is up from 147 in 2009, when this book was first conceived.

2.2 WORKING IN A COMPLEX ENVIRONMENT

Over the years, the global marketplace has changed a lot. Factories in Europe and the United States have been closed down. Right now, the Western economy is increasingly powered by service provision. Manufacturing is outsourced to Asia and Africa. Even 'basic' service operations, such as call centers and ICT helpdesks, have been moved to these locations. Shell, the oil Company, for instance, has operated ICT call centers in a number of locations for years, which are available 24/7 to employees. An ICT employee in India can take control of the computer of someone in Washington D.C. to solve a problem.

And not only production has shifted. Innovation also happens globally, with South-Koreans Samsung succesfully challenging Apples lead the Smartphone martket. With the heralded introduction of 3D-printing, we are about to see a new revolution that will

28

make cheap production available everywhere, even in your own house.

The work that remains is of a high-quality and complex nature. Consequently, more and more demands are placed on employees. There is a rise in the average level of training of employees and it is becoming ever more important for employees to continue to learn new skills and develop existing ones. People are faced with having to solve progressively more complex problems, problems with more and more different sides to them. And employees are expected to know all about these different sides and take them into account when tackling the problems at hand.

Reducing complexity
Organizations still try to solve the issue of increasing complexity by trying to bring this complexity down to a tangible and measurable level. The eighties saw a large-scale implementation of quality systems aimed at dealing with this complexity, reducing it to 'critical processes' or 'critical success factors'. The rationale behind this was that, if these factors were identified, they could be managed, and all would be well. A large number of companies and governments introduced these types of systems: ISO certification and HACCP, among others. This is called quality-management.

This so-called quality management has been implemented on a grand scale and can be found across all branches of business. And new quality management systems are still being designed, Unfortunately, it turns out that these systems are unable to prevent new problems from occurring. Whenever a new problem arises, a new variant is added to the quality system, which does not take care of the underlying complexity. In time quality management systems become as complex as the complexity they are trying te reduce.

Here are some examples from the previous decades, starting with one case where disaster never actually even struck:

- The 'Year2000' bug prompted organizations to draw up plans to detect the bug as well as emergency plans in case of equipment failure. These plans included waking people up with megaphones if, as a result of a power failure, doorbells were no longer working.
- Companies listed on a stock exchange introduced a corporate governance code following the Enron accounting scandal.
- Many companies introduced social media policies to govern how their people use social media like Twitter, Facebook and LinkedIn after somebody wrote a negative comment about the company online.
- Hospitals introduced several registration systems to prevent medical errors, following several mistakes.

The thought behind these measures is positive: that people learn from their mistakes and adapt their plans and methods of working.

The main issue, however, is that all of these measures rest on the central belief that reality is makeable and manageable. The measures are implemented from the view that organizations are as machines that, when one part breaks down, can be fixed. The management systems only look at the parts in the whole and try to find a suitable solution for these parts individually. Very few management experts look at the organization as a whole and any interrelations between the parts are also ignored. Actions are based on a fragmented instead of a holistic approach.

The big danger in this way of thinking is that the systems end up taking on a life of their own and are no longer controlled by the people who operate them. The system is elevated to being the standard, compliance to the rules of the (quality)system becomes more important than trying something new. Anything outside and non-compliant to the system is seen as risky, so people will not even attempt it. Employees are given very little room to take own initiatives. Creativity and experiment is no longer valued in daily work, but restricted to the research and development department.

As a result, employees hide behind processes, systems, their duties and job profile. Highly trained professionals have very little freedom to operate autonomously and the organization loses a lot of time maintaining their quality systems. Employees no longer feel a sense of enjoyment in their work, and can become disoriented and demoralized. The connection between employees and what they do is lost. Consequently, employees feel less involved in their work. Loss of involvement leads to a decline in quality, whereas the introduction of the quality systems was actually intended to manage and improve quality!

2.3 NOT ONLY COMPLEXITY

The world around us is not only getting more complex, but things are changing faster too. Technology is developing at an increasingly faster rate, with new possibilities emerging around us almost daily. There are smartphones that can help us in every aspect of our life through apps. Businesses are faced with new online technologies such as Social Media, which should be taken into account when going online with a product or service. But consumers are changing faster too. The Internet started the revolution by allowing access to more and more information so that consumers could make their own choices. Nowadays, consumers have access to up-to-date price information through social media and review sites, and they can switch between services easily.

All these changes lead to turbulence and time pressure for organizations. In a turbulent world, an organization receives new information almost all the time. This information can have consequences for the organization. If we look at making a new product, an organization can no longer separate between the phases of designing, building, testing, and analyzing the product. New information can influence the design even when the product is almost finished. Therefore, the different phases have to be performed at the same time or in small steps that follow each other quickly, which is called an iterative cycle. The benefit is that information gained during testing can easily be used to create a better design, without 'going back to the drawing board' and erasing the previous hard work.

Because things are changing faster, time pressure is becoming a bigger issue. Time pressure affects people because they gain a **sense of urgency** in dealing with a project. Likewise, complexity leads to feelings of **ambiguity** when there are too many options to consider. Turbulence leads to feelings of **uncertainty** when you don't know what will happen next.

Improvisation can help you deal with these feelings. When faced with ambiguity, improvisation teaches you to act first and make sense of your action when you know the outcome. Uncertainty becomes bearable because you can always use the new information in the next iterative cycle. Finally, improvisation can tackle a sense of urgency because it speeds up tasks by letting you think while you act.

Advantages

Scientific research has uncovered even more advantages of improvisation in organizations, besides helping you cope with uncertainty, ambiguity and time pressure. For example, scientists found that using improvisation while developing new products leads to more successful products and allows people to learn more in the process. Improvisation helps you to make sense of a problem and increases the problem solving skills and self mastery of the professional. Succeful problem solving increases motivation, and if everybody in a team has these feelings, teamwork also increases. Look at the textbox on the next page for a fictional example of how improvisation helps all these processes.

2.4 ORGANIZING FOR IMPROVISATION

In the example, improvisation almost seems too good to be true, but the advantages of improvisation can really be achieved, although it doesn't happen automatically. Improvisation has to be organized for; it has to be organized for on both a cultural and

At the company Beans & Co, a new product development team is working on a new coffeemaker that can make luxury coffee for a low price. Everything goes as planned and the team works according to their normal processes of planning first and acting later.

The team leader then receives a report that one of their competitors is almost ready to introduce a similar product. What's more, the competitor's product has some additional features that theirs doesn't have. At this point, the team leader decides that improvisation is the best course of action: to introduce their product first and develop additional features as they go along. The team leader conveys his sentiments to his team and they start improvising. One person is testing the machine by putting pads into place and turning the machine on. While doing this, he discovers he can do it faster by leaving the lid half open and sliding the pads into place without having to open and close the lid. A second person sees this and quickly devises an automatic inserting system so that people only have to push one button if they want coffee. The team is so enthusiastic about this that they all become more motivated and start working together more and combining ideas.

Because of the time pressure, the team uses an injection molding technique to make their machine, instead of assembling parts. This technique is later carried over into the actual production and is implemented on the factory floor.

At the end of a frantic period of development, the team has produced a new coffeemaker with just one button, two weeks ahead of schedule. They are better motivated and have achieved an insight which is also valuable to another part of the organization: production.

structural level. To show that improvisation can be implemented in many environments, we'll look at two totally different organizations: *Google* and the *German army*.

Organizational culture

Improvisation on a cultural level gives you an experimental culture, where failure is accepted and people are given freedom to act. Improvisation also allows an organization to develop a mind-set of determination and resilience, as they know they can face what the world throws at them.

Accepting failure sounds like a bad idea, but what it means is that competent mistakes have to be tolerated or even promoted. Competent mistakes are mistakes that are born out of novel ideas and not out of bad execution. At 21 Lobsterstreet, we call this a *nearling* (see also www.nearling.com). A nearling is a positive word for something new that you did with the right intentions, which has not (yet) led to the right result. Calling something a nearling emphasizes that initiatives are almost *always* valuable, even if they don't lead to the right result (directly).

Some reasons why nearlings are important for organizations, and why employees should be proud of them, are:
- You started an initiative.
- You may have moved others.
- Maybe it led you to something that was successful.
- Many nearlings go before a few successes.
- You learned from it.

Google encourages mistakes, not only small mistakes, but also very big ones, as the following example at the right page from an article in *Fortune* magazine shows.

Freedom to act is another important part of improvisation on a cultural level. People need to have the freedom — and also the responsibility — to act as they think is best. Google puts this into practice by giving every employee 20% of their time to work on projects that they want to do. Google also explicitly states on their

Take the case of Sheryl Sandberg, a 37-year-old vice president whose responsibility includes the company's automated advertising system. Sandberg recently committed an error that cost Google several million dollars — "Bad decision, moved too quickly, no controls in place, wasted some money," is all she'll say about it — and when she realized the magnitude of her mistake, she walked across the street to inform Larry Page, Google's co-founder and unofficial thought leader. "God, I feel really bad about this," Sandberg told Page, who accepted her apology. But as she turned to leave, Page said something that surprised her. "I'm so glad you made this mistake," he said. "Because I want to run a company where we are moving too quickly and doing too much, not being too cautious and doing too little. If we don't have any of these mistakes, we're just not taking enough risk."

Source Fortune, Vol. 154, No. 7, October 2, 2006, by Adam Lashinsky.

recruitment website that they *"listen to every idea, on the theory that any Googler can come up with the next breakthrough."* While Google is the most well-known company that uses free time as a way to innovate, there are a lot of other companies that do this. HP and 3M for example started with this back in the 1940's.

Another, more unlikely, place to find this culture is the army. The German army, from when it was still the Prussian army in the 1800s to the modern day, uses what is called *Auftragstaktik[1]*. This strategy has been followed by other armies, including NATO, under the name of 'mission command.' In *Auftragstaktik*, subordinates are not given orders to follow, but rather a goal which they must achieve. This is an important difference, as the subordinate can choose how he will accomplish that goal himself. In contrast, when following orders, someone higher in the hierarchy decides how a subordinate should act.

The **mind-set** of improvising organizations is one of determination and resilience. Determination, because people and organizations need to go on when faced with adversity. If you just quit when something is not going your way, success will be far off. But resilience, or the ability to bounce back from adversity, comes with an improvisational mind-set. When you know you can improvise your way out of a hard spot, you won't be as afraid of adversity. Hence the saying *'when life gives you lemons, make lemonade.'*

Organizational structure

On a structural level, organizational improvisation teaches us to use a minimal structure. Improvisation is not uncontrolled chaos; it does need a structure in order to occur. This can be seen in both jazz and theatrical improv. The structure of a song is the framework in which jazz musicians can freely improvise and let their creativity flow. Improv actors use similar structures, called games, that provide a shared understanding of the possibilities, limitations and the goal of the scene that is being improvised.

In business, **minimal structures** can be achieved through invisible controls. Invisible, or indirect, controls are controls which do not restrict the creativity and spontaneity of improvisation. Indirect control can be exercised by people themselves, through shared values, ethics, and social pressure. Following rules can be advantageous, but people should always be able to able to discard a rule if it is no longer relevant. In armies that use *Auftragstaktik*, subordinates are even allowed the extreme action of disobeying an officer if it serves the established goal.

From this example, we see that a **clear goal** is important. A goal should be clear to everyone involved and, more importantly, the *intent* of the goal should be understood by everybody. A clear goal provides the direction for an organization to work towards. The goal might even change during the process, to adapt to new ideas, but it must remain clear to everybody. Short-term milestones, such as deadlines or testing versions of a product, can be another form of indirect control as they force people to work toward a certain target, without telling them how to achieve it.
A good way to formulate a goal is to define a BHAG (pronounced bee-hag), a *Big, Hairy, Audacious Goal.* James Collins and Jerry

Porras invented this acronym in 1996 as a way to challenge organizations to come up with visionary and emotionally compelling goals. A BHAG is very suited to improvisation, as it gives people a unifying focal point, without detailing how it should be reached. Google's BHAG, for example, is to *"organize the world's information and make it universally accessible and useful."* Another good example is Twitter's BHAG: "To become the pulse of the planet." Notice that these goals are motivating, but leave room for other ways to achieve them, even outside the company's core business.

To keep the goal clear to everybody, communication is key. The improvisation process moves forward when everybody communicates regularly. If people are aware of each other's progress, they can help each other with ideas and insights. Fluid communication gives everybody **real-time information** on the project. This can be used to spot problems and opportunities as soon as they occur. People will be able to act before situations become too problematic.

Real-time information comes not only from within a project, but also from the environment around people. This was the main reason for the Prussian army to implement *Auftragstaktik*. As war is a messy, complex and dynamic activity, soldiers need to be able to react in the moment. If they encounter a problem, they have the real-time information on the situation at hand. If they have to stop and wait for instructions on how to deal with the situation, it is probably too late (which can have deadly consequences).

Soldiers therefore improvise on the information presented to them. Officers who are removed from the battlefield have other real-time information presented to them and are able to see the big picture. They improvise upon this bigger picture by passing along the relevant information to soldiers in the field — not as orders, but as warning signals and guidelines that the soldier can combine with his own insights to decide on an action.

PART 2
PROFES-
SIONAL
SKILLS

In this part we focus on the professional skills that are linked to improvisation. We explained the four sides of improvisation in the previous part, framing it in the personal and professional domain. The skills of an improv actor are the same skills that a professional in the workplace can use. In the following chapters, we will be exploring topics such as leadership, creativity and multicultural teams. Some skills are essential for each of these topics. We call them the 7 Habits of Great Improvisers.

THE 7 HABITS OF
GREAT IMPROVISERS

1 - Say Yes, And...

The first lesson that an improviser learns is to accept every offer that is made. This basic rule is known as 'Yes, anding.' This principle allows improvisers to be positive and always look for new directions and opportunities. By saying 'yes,' you accept an idea 'and' you develop the idea further, making it better. An idea will quickly grow if you're positive.

2 - Be Flexible

An improviser never really knows what he will be confronted with, so he should not be too fixated on following his own plan. He has to be willing to abandon his own ideas and go along with other people's. Flexibility also helps to create new associations and connections.

3 - Be in the Moment

A great improviser lives in the here and now, in the present. He is alert and is able to respond instantly and sharply to changes or sudden twists and turns. This means that he is not distracted by all sorts of other thoughts, but that he is totally focused on things that are happening around him at that particular moment in time. By being in the present, and not judging the situation, all options are open and everything is possible.

4 - Experiment

Before they start doing anything, great improvisers focus on the big picture. The details will follow spontaneously once they start improvising and experimenting. If you want to plan all the details in advance, you will spend a lot of time only to discover that reality is more resilient than you thought. It is only through experimentation that you will find out what does and doesn't work.

5 - Follow your Intuition

By being in the here and now and by not following a preconceived path, the improviser has to rely on his intuition. Often, he does not know in advance what he will do, or why he does something, but he does it because he trusts his intuition. Combining intuition with discipline is a promising combination in business.

6 - Make Others Look Good

A good improviser is very altruistic by nature. One of the ground rules of improv is: make sure the other person is having a good time. When you watch two improvisers on stage, you can easily see this habit at work. They make sure the other person looks good. They do not try to outshine the other person.

7 - Dare to Fail

It's very important that a great improviser dares to fail. It is the opposite of trying to prevent every mistake. If you try to control the whole situation, you end up spending more time and money instead of making the mistake and learning from it. And learning from mistakes is a vital part of improvising too. So go for it, fail fast and learn fast.

LEADING TEAM IMPRO- VISATION

CHAPTER 3

Within organizations, improvisation most easily flourishes on a team level, as it does in the theater and in jazz. We can learn a lot from the techniques that theatrical improvisers use to create a scene on stage. Some techniques that we discussed in chapter 1 can immediately translate to teams. They are 'yes, anding,' 'making the others look good,' and 'being in the moment.'

3.1 TEAM IMPROVISATION

It is important for teamwork that the team members experience a feeling of trust and know that their ideas will be accepted by their fellow team members. Trust is enhanced by using the 7 Habits of Great Improvisers, most of all Yes, Anding, being in the moment, and making the other person look good.

'**Yes, anding**,' is the first step in fostering trust. 'Yes, and' means you accept another person's suggestion and then build on the suggestion to make it better. The opposite of 'Yes, and' is 'Yes, but.' 'Yes, but,' unfortunately, is one of the most common reactions to an idea. Saying 'Yes, but' kills an idea very quickly, destroying the positive energy of the person who thought of the idea. More on 'Yes, but' and idea killers can be found in chapter 4 on creativity.

Trust is further enhanced by trying to **make the others look good**. When improvising, you want to be able to experiment and take risks to try new ideas. This opens up the possibility that you will fail. But, as we discussed earlier in chapter 2, making mistakes isn't bad. And when you have fellow team members trying to help you, they will help you turn the failure into a success.

The third habit is **being in the moment**. This technique makes it possible for team members to 'Yes, and' each other and integrate unexpected events into their everyday work. Being in the moment is the individual equivalent of real-time information and communication on an organizational level.

If a sufficient level of teamwork is reached, teams even develop a 'feel' for each other; they instinctively know how other team members are going to react and they can act upon this instinct. This is how great improv teams manage to make improv look so effortless.

Building a team
The make-up of the team is also important for effective organizational improvisation. The most important factors are diversity

and size. Teams can have diverse cultural, functional and personal characteristics. The importance of multi-cultural teams and how to handle them is presented extensively in chapter 5. Functional and personal diversity are important because they give a team a broad repertoire of skills, knowledge and experience to build upon. This leads to many different ideas that can be combined to form smart, out-of-the-box solutions to challenges. Google not only makes functionally diverse teams, but also requires the employees themselves to have a broad knowledge base. One of their requirements for new employees is that they *"have broad knowledge and expertise in many different areas of computer science and mathematics."*

The size of a team is also important. Small teams are generally more favorable for improvisation. In theatrical improv, teams almost always consist of four people. In business, the ideal number of people seems to lie between 6 and 8. This allows for a lot of diversity without hampering direct communication between team members. On Google's recruitment page, they say: *"We work in small teams to promote spontaneity, creativity, and speed."*

3.2 IMPROVISATIONAL LEADERSHIP

Another, very important aspect of teamwork is the role of the leader. How should a leader act in order to increase the quality of improvisation? Is a leader even necessary, or will it just hamper improvisation?

Scientific research shows that, yes, a leader is beneficial for improvisation. But not all leaders have a positive effect on improvisation and the leader does not always need to be the same person the entire time. A directive leader, for example, whose main focus is controlling and commanding people, will squash improvisation in almost any team. This is because improvisation requires both control and freedom. The challenge of leading improvisation is to combine these conflicting demands. This is difficult, but not impossible.

Freedom and control oppose each other, and so the logical thing to say is that they cannot be combined. Trying to combine two opposites anyway is called a paradox because it is impossible to do

ROUND THE CLOCK: A REAL WORLD EXAMPLE OF IMPROVISATIONAL LEADERSHIP

At the end of the previous millennium, Iberomoldes, a leading company in the molding industry, pioneered global teamwork in a virtual environment by using new computer software. This project, called Round The Clock, brought together teams from Portugal, Mexico and China in order to be able to develop a new product 24 hours per day. The assignment was to create a 3D model using new software. Each team would work on the project during their work hours and at the end of the day (which was the beginning of the day for the team in another time zone) the two teams would contact each other to explain their progress and design choices. This project was observed by Associate Professor Pina e Cunha and his team and resulted in a live

demonstration to the Portuguese prime minister.

The team leader was the CEO of Iberomoldes, Joaquim Menezes. Menezes was very passionate about the project and believed the best chance to succeed was to experiment with the new computer software until good protocols were reached. At first he gave his engineers and IT experts free rein to experiment as they saw fit. This resulted in a four-week process where team members would leisurely try new approaches and software in order to learn about their pros and cons. At the end of the four-week testing period, they reached the conclusion that the first system they tested was still the best system.

Frustrated by the lack of apparent process, Menezes decided to raise the stakes and ask the engineers around the world to come up with a new product before a set deadline. He made it clear that this test was very important for the continuity of the product. He did not, however, specify how the goal was to be reached, but allowed his team to come up with their own methods of working.

Although the system did not always work, the engineers felt compelled to make it work in order to make the deadline. Instead of looking for new software when they encountered negative effects, they designed simple fixes to work around the effects. The audio would sometimes cut out, and when that happened they improvised by writing on a piece of paper and showing it to the other team through the webcam. Because of a lag in voice communication, the teams would frequently interrupt and talk over each other. The simple solution was to introduce military radio commands such as 'over.'

This example shows us that a combination of control (a non-negotiable deadline) and freedom (letting the team devise the methods of working) was necessary for successful improvisation.

Source Pina e Cunha, Kamoche & Campos e Cunha, Organizational improvisation and leadership: A field study in two computer mediated settings, 2003.

two things that contradict each other at the same time. However, it is possible to find a third way where you do one thing that has the same effect as doing the two contradicting things at the same time. This is called a synthesis.

Improvisation itself is also a synthesis. It brings together planning and acting. By improvising, you constantly alternate between planning and acting. Planning gives you information on how you should act, and by acting you obtain more information on how to proceed. When improvising, planning and acting alternate so fast that they blur together. That's why improvisation has the effects of planning and acting simultaneously. The synthesis between freedom and control can be found in two leadership styles: servant leadership and rotating leadership. Each of these two leadership styles gives a team and its leader the means to combine freedom and control.

3.3 SERVANT LEADERSHIP

Servant leaders lead by putting themselves below their team members, rather than above them. They want to get the best out of the team members they lead and will put the needs of the team above their own needs. A servant leader leads by influencing people through the following activities:
- Establishing a vision
- Building credibility
- Building trust
- Giving service

A vision is an image of a positive future that the leader wants to achieve. A leader develops vision by making sense of patterns and trends as they unfold. A servant leader uses a vision to inspire and motivate people to act towards that future. Robert Greenleaf, who first proposed servant leadership, calls this 'change by convincement.'

How to build credibility is explained in the book The Leadership Challenge by Kouzes and Posner. In short, a leader should:
1. Know himself
2. Appreciate his people
3. Affirm shared values
4. Be (seen as) capable
5. Be useful
6. Create and sustain hope

If a leader is seen as credible, he can start building trust. Not only should his people trust him, but he should also work on building trust in order to get people to trust themselves and each other. A servant leader does not focus on the end result, but on building trust and trusting his people to come up with a good solution. A servant leader knows his people will deliver a great end result if he focuses on allowing them to do their work well.

He achieves this by giving service. Giving service can be done by taking on easy or repetitive tasks so that the team members can focus on the more important tasks. Service can also be simply asking a lot of questions. Through these questions, a team member can discover things on his own, instead of being told what to do. The team member will come to feel that a problem is his problem and be more motivated to solve it.

A servant leader shares some of the 7 Habits of Great Improvisers. First of all, a servant leader is **positive**. He creates and sustains hope and appreciates his people. Appreciating his people can also be seen as **making the other look good**, which is coupled with giving service to his people so they can shine. He is **in the moment** as he has a focus on the process. **Experimenting, following his intuition, being flexible** and **allowing others to fail** are not necessarily characteristics of a servant leader, but they do proceed from his positive attitude.

Giving freedom
As you can see from these activities, a servant leader gives a lot of freedom to his people so that they can perform to the best of their abilities. But sometimes people cannot or will not perform to their utmost. In this case a leader has to step in. The pitfall, however, would be to take away the freedom and replace it by control. Instead, a servant leader has the ability to steer people without making them lose the feeling of freedom. A servant leader can do this with invisible controls, or controls that don't feel like controls.

Questions can be very controlling — while still allowing freedom in the answer. If a servant leader thinks a product should be blue, he can ask the team member: "Do you think this product should be light blue or dark blue?" If a team member responds with: "I don't know if this product should be blue at all," the servant leader can give him the
reason why blue is the better color in the form of another question. "If blue has been proven to calm people, why should we use another color for our calming product?" This question still leaves room for the team member to disagree, but only by reasoning. If the reasons are good enough, the servant leader should be open enough to give in.

There are many other methods for a servant leader to come up with invisible controls. One is to control the actions of an unwilling or incapable team member indirectly, by asking other team members to help him or give him advice. If a team member is postponing an important task, take over the task he is currently doing so that he will focus on the important task.

Robert Greenleaf developed his views on servant leadership after he retired as Director of Management Research at AT&T in the 1960s. He was greatly influenced by Journey to the East, a short story by Nobel Prize winner Hermann Hesse. The essence of that story is as follows.

Among a traveling band of adventurers on a mythical journey to the East, Leo is a menial servant of chores, spirit, and song. A while into the journey, Leo disappears, and the group falls into disarray and the journey is abandoned. Years later, the narrator discovers that Leo the servant was in fact the head of the Order that had commissioned the journey: the lowly servant was in fact, its guiding spirit, a great and noble leader.

From Leo's journey, and sixty years of his own experience, Greenleaf concluded that the meaning of the story was that great leaders must first serve others.

3.4 ROTATING LEADERSHIP

The second leadership style that can make the synthesis between freedom and control is rotating leadership. Rotating leadership can also be called team leadership. In rotating leadership, there is not one single leader, but everyone can take control of the process as they see fit. In jazz, leadership of the song that is played shifts from one musician to the next. Usually there is a solo by one musician, and at the end of that solo the other musicians follow the soloist's lead in developing the song further, until a new musician takes the lead. In improvisational theatre, the focus can shift from performer to performer as the scene progresses. It is the role of the other performers to support this focus and build on the input of the performer who has the focus.

In organizations, the person with the best capabilities to handle a certain situation will become the leader. When a new situation arises, another team member can take over the leadership role. Rotating leadership helps improvisation because it gives all the team members the ability to control the process, but allows them the freedom to experiment as well.

If other team members also take the leadership role, the person who normally has the leadership role can help the team by taking up a role as a team member. Besides being a team member, he can also help by facilitating the team. For example, he can make sure that only relevant information reaches them, and that the team has a clear, dynamic goal.

Rotating leadership works best when people know what the other team members are good at. Leadership is not handed over formally, but switches naturally when someone puts an idea forward, gives feedback to others or starts working on a new project. If all the team members know each other's capabilities, the leadership shift can be anticipated. This might be as simple as looking towards the IT expert when there is a computer problem, but in teams where

Consider how improvisation and rotating leadership helped FastTrack, a company that develops and produces high-tech products and that was studied by Professor Anne Miner. One of the improvisations that Professor Miner's team observed was cutting search time in one of their programs from 22 to 2 seconds by fixing an unrelated bug. A marketer took over leadership and suggested that this could be marketed as a unique selling point. Under his temporary leadership, the engineer built a speedy reporting feature based on the information search.

many people have the same function, the differences in expertise are more subtle.

In teams that know each other and are familiar with each other's strengths and weaknesses, trust has usually developed over time, allowing the team to communicate very quickly. In these teams, the leadership shift has become almost automatic as the team accepts the capabilities of the person taking charge and team members are willing to temporarily abandon their own claim to leadership as someone else steps up.

A team that practices rotating leadership has all the 7 Habits of Great Improvisers. They **make the others look good** by letting them take over leadership when necessary. They do this **intuitively** and **flexibly** and while staying **in the moment**. Team members can **experiment**, because the other team members will take over leadership and help out in case it goes wrong. And, as we'll discuss shortly, **positivity** is key for rotating leadership.

Reaching rotating leadership
When a team doesn't have much experience together, when they are not willing to accept people as temporary leaders, or when team members are afraid to step up and take the leadership, rotating leadership will not work. Sometimes this can be solved by agreeing on some ground rules, as jazz or theater improvisers do. These ground rules would be to allow each team member to take leadership, to have a shared responsibility for the work process and to help each other so that everybody feels safe to make a worthwhile addition to the process. Ofcourse these ground rules have to be practised. Try using some of the exercises in the toolbox for this.

Rotating leadership has the best effects on improvisation, even better then servant leadership. But if a new team is struggling to implement rotating leadership, servant leadership is a way of slowly easing into rotating leadership. If a team has an official team leader, they can start out with the official leader taking the servant leader role. The other team members can then use rotating leadership among themselves. The servant leader's task is to guide this process. As this way of working becomes more and more natural, the servant leader can spend less time facilitating and more time joining in on the work. In the end, the whole team will be working according to the principles of rotating leadership.

Positivity & ownership

No matter which leadership style is chosen, it is important that the leader and the team stay positive: in other words, that they keep watching for opportunities and remain willing to act on them. A positive attitude helps improvisation, as it determines how team members react to the uncertainty that is part of improvisation. A positive attitude makes team members regard uncertainty as an opportunity, rather than a threat.

If negativity sets in in a team, two things can happen. Everybody might retreat to their own task and stop communicating, or people might start arguing and even sabotaging the others. Potentially advantageous opportunities or potentially dangerous problems will be ignored because 'someone else will deal with it.' It is therefore important that leaders keep giving team members a sense of ownership of the project at hand. Leaders have a responsibility to stay positive, as their mood has a large effect on the group. Servant leadership puts a leader in a natural positive mood, as his goal is to make things better for the team members. If a team leader has difficulty acting like a servant leader, being positive is a great way to start.

CREATIVE THINKING

CHAPTER 4

In this chapter we start with a definition of creative thinking and give several reasons why creative thinking is so important in these times. Creativity can be seen as a general skill, but you can also pursue applied creative thinking, so you learn ways of stimulating your brain to generate loads of creative ideas. You will see that many of the 7 Habits of Great Improvisers can be applied to the domain of creative thinking. You need an open attitude, because being positive and flexible is absolutely essential for coming up with new ideas. You need to experiment and to dare to fail because you won't find the right ideas and answers immediately. We will give an overview of the most important skills and explain the creative process.

4.1 WHAT IS CREATIVE THINKING?

There are several definitions of creativity. Therefore, it is important to clarify which meaning we associate with creativity:

Creativity refers to the phenomenon whereby a person creates something new (a product, a solution, a work of art, a novel, a joke, etc.) that has some kind of value.[3]

If we study this in a little more detail and zoom in on the concept by focusing our attention on creative thinking, the following definition provides an apt framework:

Creative thinking is the total sum of thinking behaviors, skills, techniques, and processes which increase the chance of breaking patterns, establishing new connections in our brain.[3]

So it is about breaking certain thinking patterns: patterns we acquired as a result of our upbringing, our educational system, our groups of friends, our working environment, our culture, worldviews, etc. Our brains are good at making and using patterns. If we have been successful at doing something once, chances are that we will follow the same 'route' when we are presented with a similar problem or question. Just think for a moment which way you normally take to school or work. You probably take the same way every time.

Now see if you can recognize a few more patterns in your everyday life: do you have a certain morning ritual? Do you follow certain procedures at school or work to tackle particular problems? Do you find yourself ordering the same dish in your favorite restaurant? These are all questions you have probably answered yes to. Just as well, really. Because if we had to come up with a new process or method for every single thing we are confronted with on a daily basis, we would end up wasting a lot of time and being very inefficient. So it is a good thing that our brains create patterns which help us to survive the hectic craziness of everyday living.

[2]Definition: Wikipedia, the online encyclopedia: http://en.wikipedia.org/wiki/Creativity
[3]Definition: Creativity Today by Igor Byttebier and Ramon Vullings

But there are some instances where we want to break these patterns because they are no longer efficient or effective, as shown by the following situations:

- We are looking for solutions, ideas, opportunities beyond logic. The logical route does not seem to work anymore and we need to come up with another solution. For example: as an organization, you wish to think about the future of your company in 2050. Logical ideas will not be of very much use to you as they build on your knowledge of things as they are now. So, you have to abandon logic and allow your mind to dream and fantasize freely about all sorts of possibilities. Thanks to creativity, you will be able to build up a picture.

- We want to create new combinations or establish original connections between two — at first glance — totally different areas. For instance: you want to conduct your meetings in a different way because the meetings often go on too long and are boring. Using creativity, you try to find another way of meeting with each other, a way which is dynamic and exciting. You may end up with the concept of a family walk. This is also a gathering during which you discuss issues but in a much more informal and natural atmosphere. You subsequently combine these two areas (meeting with colleagues and family walk) and your outcome may be a wonderwalk - a walk with colleagues where agenda items are discussed in an organic way in small subgroups.

- We want to come out of our comfort zone to discover new opportunities. For instance: the manager of a well-performing production department in a toy company has noticed that his employees are easily satisfied and are no longer as sharp as they used to be because sales figures have been really good. To stimulate creativity, he could ask his team the following question 'What would happen if a competitor released a much better product on the market?' By doing so, he takes his employees out of their comfort zone and they are forced to think a few steps ahead to create new solutions.

- We want to leave the beaten track, consciously and in a process-oriented way. For example: for years, you have been taking the same route to work. To improve your creativity, you decide to come up with an alternate way of going to work at least once a month: you take another route, you cycle to work, you pick up a colleague who lives on the other side of town. This allows you to keep discovering new routes and places and, who knows, you may even end up somewhere you have never been before. That is when you're practicing the habit of being flexible.

Most of our everyday life is spent thinking logically and following established patterns. However, there are some situations (as described above) where we consciously use our creative thinking capacity and we are able to:
- create new products and services;
- develop processes, methods and people;
- change the world.

4.2 THE IMPORTANCE OF CREATIVE THINKING

Ten to fifteen years ago, a lot of companies still considered creativity quite a vague concept in the business world. It was something intangible, something related to art, a buzzword which looked good on corporate mission statements. A lot of people and organizations viewed creativity a little suspiciously and were unsure about how to apply a creative process in practice.

These days, however, creativity has become serious business. The power of creative thinking is recognized more and more often. In many cases, it has even become a necessary means for survival in this competitive world where organizations are faced with having to outsource production to countries with cheap labor, with a wealth of technological advances so everything has to happen faster, more efficiently, at better quality, where consumers are becoming ever more critical and vocal, systems are increasingly more complex, internationalization continues to increase,

60

and you find yourself having to compete at an ever higher level. All of these issues (and there are undoubtedly many more) mean that people and organizations have to deal with the world (processes, structures, people, products, services) in different ways. And in order to do this, you will have to break down certain thinking patterns. You will have to introduce creative thinking because simply delivering good quality and providing fast service is no longer enough. Organizations have to constantly question and innovate themselves.

Considering the evolution over the past few years and looking ahead, we predict that creative thinking will become a very important skill in the coming decades — be it in relation to practical matters (e.g. coming up with ideas for a new product or service) or social developments in the world (e.g. traffic jam problems, environmental issues, intercultural integration.) This hypothesis is supported on various levels: the amount of attention Richard Florida has gotten following the publication of his book *The Rise of the Creative Class*; the government-led initiatives in Belgium and the Netherlands (innovation awards, foundation of the Flanders District of Creativity;) the overwhelming success of creative organizations such as Google.

4.3 APPLIED CREATIVITY

This is all good and well. Nice to know that creativity is important and that you can do a lot with it, but the question now, of course, is how you go about stimulating creativity. One answer may be that creativity emerges naturally as long as you are patient. Your subconscious eventually produces a solution or idea if it finds the problem interesting and challenging enough to work on it while you're not paying attention. (This is called the incubation method — the term incubation is also used to refer to the hatching period of birds' eggs.) Often, however, we do not have the time or patience to wait for these ideas to emerge. In this case, it is more useful to work with creativity models and techniques which may serve as a catalyst for innovative ideas and concepts. In this chapter, we review some of these models, focus on a number of basic skills involved in creative thinking and discuss the different steps in a creative process.

4.4 SKILLS INVOLVED IN CREATIVE THINKING

You need a number of skills in order to develop your creative thinking capacity. These skills align very well with the 7 Habits of Great Improvisers. The five key skills are:

- Creative perception
- Suspension of judgment
- Free association
- Divergent thinking
- Imagination

1 Creative perception We perceive things using our senses. The senses filter the external stimuli we receive from the world around us. The external sensations are subsequently colored by our mind-set. These patterns were formed as a result of our upbringing, education, values, beliefs, life experience, etc. In this way, every person creates their own perception of reality. It follows that, if we can change our patterns, we can also change our perception of the world. Within creativity, this is a very important process because you want to perceive things from different angles so you can come up with different solutions as a result. Training yourself in creative perception — in other words, learning to look at the world from a different perspective — allows you to break free from existing views and patterns because you are able to see an alternate reality.

2 Suspension of judgment Suspension of judgment is one of the most important and probably one of the most difficult basic rules in the creative process. In everyday life, we are constantly making judgments. The minute we get out of bed, we are faced with having to make decisions which involve having to make judgments (what outfit to wear, what to have for breakfast, what time to leave for work.) We have become so good at making judgments that we are no longer aware we are even doing it.

When we are confronted with new or different situations, ideas or views which deviate from our existing thinking patterns, we feel uncomfortable, and at first tend to judge them negatively. As a result, the new idea is not explored and developed further.

By consciously suspending your judgment, and accepting all of your own and other people's ideas, you will be more open to those with other ideas, other views, and other solutions. You will see more options, increasing the chance of there being really original and useful ideas among the alternative ideas conceived.

3 Free association We associate things with each other by linking one thought with another. In principle, a starting thought may lead you to thousands of other thoughts. But, here too, patterns (acquired through upbringing, education, friends) will cause certain associations to emerge more quickly. When you think about the word 'euro', your first thought is probably money. This association, by the way, has only emerged since the introduction of the euro. Prior to this, you would probably have thought about something totally different. These days, your thoughts may include: currency, Europe, Brussels, the Eurovision song contest.

The power of free association is that you go one step beyond your first associative thought. In a creative process, the idea is to establish a new connection. This can be done in two ways, dissociation and resociation.

- In a dissociation, you consciously try to 'escape' from the normal thinking pattern. If we take the example of the word 'euro', then a dissociation could be 'cow'. Cow and euro seemingly have nothing in common at first glance. In a dissociation, you consciously jump to the next, obscure step.
- In a resociation, you try to connect two totally different things with each other. You start off in a different field and then establish a reconnection with the known path. In the example above, you try to connect 'cow' with 'euro', which may lead you, for instance, to Euro Shopper brand milk.

63

4 Divergent thinking People will often stop generating ideas once one alternative is available. Divergent thinking is the ability to not stop at whatever idea you come across first. This means that you delay the tendency to stop coming up with ideas after the first wave of ideas, and go on to initiate a second or third wave of ideas. There is a range of creativity techniques that can help you to continue the divergent thinking process. For a more detailed overview, we would like to refer you to the book Creativity Today by Igor Byttebier and Ramon Vullings.

5 Developing imagination People (particularly in the Western world) are very strong in using verbal language, while imaginative skills are considerably less well-developed. Nevertheless, we all know the expression: a picture is worth a thousand words. Using your imagination refers to the ability to form a picture in your mind of something which cannot be physically perceived at that time. Examples include not just visual representations but also sounds, smells, tastes, and concepts.

Imagination allows you to make better use of your memory. After all, memories are stored in our brains as images with associated feelings. Those images can subsequently be retranslated into words to help us express ourselves. Thinking in images brings you closer to your feelings and improves creativity. Images often evoke emotions. For instance, think of a picture of a plane flying into a tower, or of your favorite team scoring the winning goal.

Imagination and emotion are very important in the creative process. Imagination also helps to evoke a clear, challenging vision of the future. Imagining things is often the first step in creating a new idea, an alternative view.

4.5 IMPROVISATION AND CREATIVITY

We devote an entire chapter on creativity because it is an inherent part of improvisation. While improvising, you use your creativity to use what your are doing and what you are experiencing to form new combinations and actions. Improvisation will become more easy as you practice your creativity. Also, you will become more creative when you improvise more. In the Toolbox, we have included several exercises that will help you train your creativity by using improvisation.

The difference between improvisation and creativity is that improvisation is always combined with action, whereas creativity can be purely conceptional. Both creativity and improvisation are part of every day actions, but can also be used as a seperate activity. For improvisation this might be a prototyping session, or a test run for a new product or service. Creativity as a seperate activity often takes the form of a creative process or brainstorm session.

4.6 THE CREATIVE PROCESS

A creative process or creative session is brought into play when a problem occurs for which there is no clear-cut solution and which requires an innovative approach. This could be about solving an existing problem or trying to identify new options and new possibilities. The important thing is that the old solution no longer works and the established thinking patterns need to be abandoned. A creative session supports this move away from existing patterns and the search for new solutions and new possibilities. Below, we have given a brief description of the three steps in the creative process and the key characteristics of each step.

Step 1. Problem definition
The problem owner is the person confronted with the problem and who is responsible for its resolution. The problem owner has to have the willingness, authority, ability, and commitment to get to work on the solutions presented to him. Although it may sometimes be difficult in practice to satisfy all four criteria, this should nevertheless be the aim. Someone may point out a problem, but if this person has no power of decision, it might be that very little will come of the innovative solutions if the actual problem owner does not give his authorization. So, at the very least, you should make sure that the person making the decisions is involved —

perhaps this person is unable to attend the entire creative session but try to at least have him there for the beginning and the end of the brainstorming session. The problem owner will then have to get to work on the chosen solutions and resolve the problem.

Briefing
At the start of the creative session, the problem owner explains what the problem is. The participants ask him questions to get a clear picture of the exact nature of the problem.

Reformulation
After the briefing, the participants are given the chance to reformulate the problem in the form of a challenge. Make sure that the phrasing of every question meets the following criteria:
- Start with 'How can I/How can we?' as this stimulates ideas.
- Be brief and to the point.
- Don't be too concrete, but don't be too abstract either.
- Make the question challenging.

Reformulation selection
The final phase of problem definition is to select one of the reformulated phrasings together with the problem owner. This will then be used in the next phases of the process.

Step 2. Divergent thinking phase (idea generation)
Using various techniques, the next phase is to excite creativity so that the participants step outside the existing frameworks and thinking patterns, and the group generates solutions and ideas. The purpose of this phase is to gather as many different ideas as possible. Every single idea has to be written down and numbered. At the end of this step, a considerable number of ideas will have been gathered. In this phase, the following rules apply:
- Suspend judgment (see section 2.4.)
- Surf along with other people's ideas.
- Promote openness in the group, privacy towards the outside world.
- Pay attention to naive ideas.
- Ideas are owned by the group.

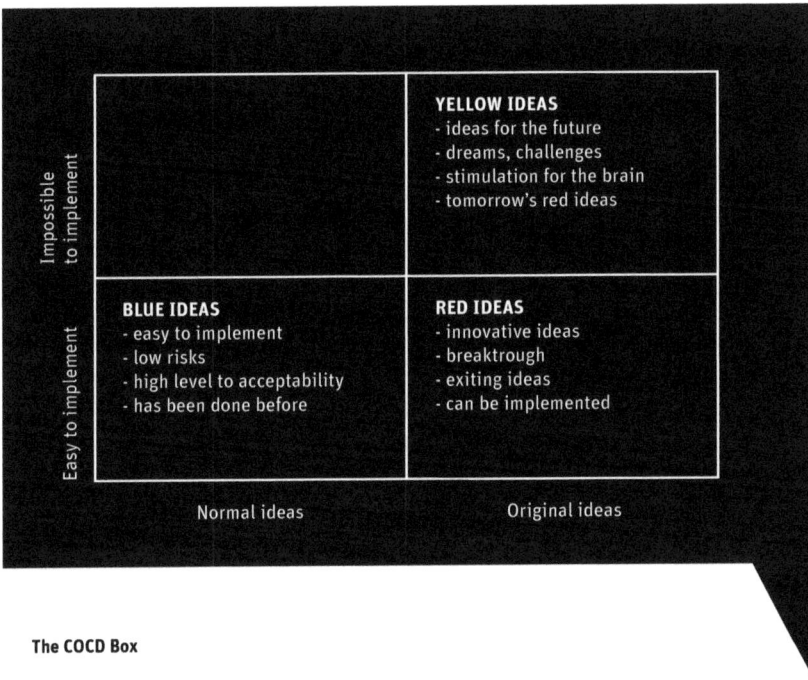

Impossible to implement			**YELLOW IDEAS** - ideas for the future - dreams, challenges - stimulation for the brain - tomorrow's red ideas
Easy to implement		**BLUE IDEAS** - easy to implement - low risks - high level to acceptability - has been done before	**RED IDEAS** - innovative ideas - breaktrough - exiting ideas - can be implemented
		Normal ideas	Original ideas

The COCD Box

Step 3. Convergent thinking phase (idea selection)

The multitude of ideas generated during the previous step is reduced to a small number. Here, too, various techniques have been developed for ensuring that innovative and promising ideas make it through the selection process. But be careful not to make choices based only on criteria such as how much money, time and people are available. The danger here is that the more creative ideas might not make it through the selection, even though the actual purpose of organizing a creative session is, in fact, to take a step beyond 'ordinary' ideas.

One very effective technique is the COCD Box. The COCD Box is a method developed by the Center for the Development of Creative Thinking (or *Centrum voor de Ontwikkeling van Creatief Denken* in Dutch, hence the abbreviation COCD.) The COCD Box is a selection method used to reduce the large number of ideas generated during the divergent thinking phase to a more manageable size. It is a means to add structure, shape and color to your chaos of ideas.

The COCD Box ensures that breakthrough ideas and future ideas are not overlooked during the convergent thinking process because they are too innovative or too progressive. This tool forces you to develop the yellow and red ideas along with the others and to include them in the final report.

Any surviving ideas are subsequently combined, further developed and improved on until concrete and usable suggestions for solutions are created. This solution then has to be implemented. This can be done by drawing up a plan of action, but also by improvising. Try out the solution in a small setting (e.g. one team or one customer) to see how it works and spread the solution, including the lessons learned by trying it, until the solution is implemented everywhere.

MULTI-CULTURAL GROUPS

CHAPTER 5

As consultants and facilitators we work a lot with culturally diverse teams. Over the years we have trained to recognize and understand cultural differences and to let these differences work in a constructive way. These differences can seem subtle but it is crucial to understand and to make space for them.

Improvisation is beneficial to multicultural groups because it helps people to appreciate each other and to use their differences constructively by saying Yes, And... to each other's different skills, attitudes and ideas.

In this chapter we explore the topic of multicultural groups. We provide some background on what we describe as a multicultural team, what works, what doesn't work, and how to lead a multicultural team. In the toolbox at the end of the book you will also find some exercises that are suitable for a multicultural setting.

5.1 GLOBALIZATION

Society is becoming more diverse, due to globalization and the widespread use of the Internet. The influence of other cultures becomes more and more evident in modern day societies. The diversity of the population is most visible in the big cities of the world. The city of Rotterdam, for example, has 174 different nationalities, London 179, and New York 170, all co-existing in a crowded city.

Not only societies have to learn to deal with cultural diversity. Organizations are also becoming more diverse. Many companies have developed a policy on Diversity and Inclusion (D&I.) Companies that use these policies try to understand and bridge the differences between different groups of employees. Many D&I policies started out to bridge differences between generations and genders. But nowadays, in a more globalized world, it becomes more and more important to be aware of cultural differences, to respect them and to use them in a positive way. Improvisation and improv games can help to get an insight into these cultural differences. The boxes on these pages show some of the topics we will look at in this chapter.

NETHERLANDS VERSUS BELGIUM

21 Lobsterstreet is an international group of professionals who work in the topics of creation, innovation and change (www.21lobsterstreet.com). We often work in the Netherlands and Flanders, the Flemish part of Belgium. Although the language in Flanders and the Netherlands is more or less the same, there are huge hidden cultural differences between the Dutch and the Flemish. In stereotypical thinking, the Dutch are perceived as blunt, to-the-point, and rude by the Flemish, and the Flemish are perceived by the Dutch as docile, unintelligent, laid back, and fond of Belgian beer and good food.

The Slang Flipchart

In order to address the differences between the Dutch and the Flemish we have developed several low-threshold interventions. One of them is the slang flipchart. During a workshop with both Flemish and Dutch participants, we collect all the typical slang or regional expressions from each language group. Any expression that is not understood by the other group is written down on the flipchart. At the end, participants try to use the other groups' way of speaking. This simple intervention gives space to language differences without making fun of the other group.

Using your own stereotype

On several occasions I (Joost Kadijk) have worked as a chair or facilitator in Flanders — sometimes as the only Dutchman in an all-Flemish group. Knowing that this can be a sensitive issue I usually make a remark or a joke about it at the start. I narrow the gap between myself and the Flemish using self-deprecating humor.

By naming and apologizing for the fact that I am the only non-Flemish person at the meeting, and having a prominent role as the facilitator, it makes it more acceptable for everyone. I use the stereotypical image that the Flemish have of the Dutch and make fun of myself.

The other way around also works well. When Cyriel (co-author and Flemish colleague) works in the Netherlands he uses the stereotypes of the Dutch about the Flemish as an icebreaker. A smart entrepreneur even used the differences between the Netherlands and Belgium as a business model for his 'Rent-a-Belgian' business. He brings Belgian enterpreneurs and scientists to Holland in order to enlarge the knowledge of the Dutch about the Belgian people's habits.

Cyriel was once booked by a Dutch firm, 'because a Flemish person talks funny,' according to the Dutch customer. So an accent can even be a reason to get hired.

5.2 WORKING WITH MULTICULTURAL TEAMS

It is important for managers to understand different cultural backgrounds, to value them, and to make them work for the team. Culture is defined and formed by complex behavior patterns and socialization in families, education, work, travel, etc. It is important to realize that every individual views the world through his or her own cultural glasses. It is also important to understand that people's behavior is based on cultural values. These values can be very different throughout a team. The challenge in multicultural teams is to appreciate and value the diversity and to create an inclusive culture instead of an exclusive culture. For this to happen, it is important to know your own background, culture, and values, the team's culture or organization's culture, and the blind spots and weaknesses.

5.3 CHARACTERISTICS OF EFFECTIVE MULTICULTURAL TEAMS

Research (by DiStefano and Adler, 2000) has shown that culturally diverse teams tend to perform worse than culturally homogeneous teams if there is no attention paid to the differences in the individual members' needs. They divide multicultural teams into three different types: destroyers, equalizers and creators.

The destroyer teams are dysfunctional because the formal leaders do not take the opinions of the team into account. When making decisions, there is no room for genuine dialogue in these teams. The equalizer teams think that they are culturally diverse and inclusive, but the team members and the leader smooth out the differences between the team members. These teams do not use the differences to their advantage.

The creator teams actively explore their differences and work like a jazz ensemble, making use of the existing differences. The more diversity there is in a team, the more possibilities there are for syn-

74

ergy. At the same time, it is difficult to achieve this synergy when the team is highly diverse. The key to success for these teams lies in the quality of the interaction processes rather than in formal team membership (Hogan, 2007).

To improve the quality of the interaction process, a multicultural group can use the 7 Habits of Great Improvisers. Here's how the 7 habits can be applied to help multicultural groups:
1. Say Yes, And... Having people from multiple cultures present, can lead to misunderstandings. Stay positive, remember that this is not because somebody has ill intent and ask for the meaning behind the action that lead to the misunderstanding.
2. Be flexible. Acknowledge that people may vary from how you expect them to act and be flexible enough to accept this and even use this new perspective to your advantage (say Yes, And...)!
3. Be in the moment. Don't focus on what other people might or might not do, but stay present to react flexibly and positively to actions.
4. Experiment. When starting up a new multicultural team, agree to experiment together to find the best way to work together. Give eachother time to achieve this.
5. Follow your intuition. Don't be too uncertain if you don't know the rules. Follow your intuition and make your intents clear.
6. Make others look good. Perhaps the most important. Help each other to understand each other. Help out when somebody is hesitant about what to do. Make the other look good by supplying insights from your culture to help the others achieve their goal.
7. Dare to fail. Sometimes it can go wrong. But use this as a learning experience. Some miscommunication is better than no communication at all.

Characteristics of an intercultural leader
It is obvious that the style of leadership influences the effectiveness of a multicultural team. A study among female leaders of multicultural teams around the world came up with the following characteristics of intercultural leaders:
1. vision and dreams with a purpose
2. winning hearts through supportive, respectful relationships;

Ethnocentric stages		
avoidance of cultural differences		
Denial	Defense	Minimization
Ethnorelative stages		
seeking out cultural differences		
Acceptance	Adaptation	Integration

Table **The developmental model of intercultural sensitivity** (Bennet and Bennett, 2004)

    solidarity
3. cultural sensitivity, promoting and celebrating differences, learning from each other and enriching life through intercultural contacts
4. leading and coaching through change and transitions
5. empowerment, tapping into the power within people
6. being a role model and a mentor

These characteristics are also the characteristics of servant leaders as described in chapter 3, specifically applied to intercultural leadership.

Ethnocentric versus ethnorelative: intercultural sensitivity
As described before, the creator teams are the most effective teams in using the cultural differences to benefit the team and its productivity. These teams are considered ethnorelative as opposed to ethnocentric. Ethnorelative teams seek out the differences and discuss them, whereas ethnocentric teams tend to avoid the cultural differences. Bennett and Bennett (2004) have developed a model of intercultural sensitivity in order to frame the differences:

The first three stages of the model are ethnocentric. People reason from their own cultural perspective, and think that the other culture does not exist (denial,) is inferior (defense,) or not important (minimization.)

In the ethnorelative stages, people see their own culture in relation to the other existing cultures. They can be seen as other possibilities and realities (acceptance,) can be used to switch perspectives when moving from one culture to another (adaptation,) or can be integrated into a new set of cultural behaviors (integration.) In this last stage, people can easily shift between different cultures, cultivate a birds' eye view, and use the diversity in different policies,

Henk van der Steen and Alieke van der Wijk (Troje Theater and training) once gave a workshop in Sri Lanka to a group of Tamil tea pickers. The group used theater to fight injustice and discrimination. A woman from Australia and a woman from Europe were also part of the team.

'We played different improv games with the group. One game included portraying different household activities.

When we shouted the word 'cooking', all the western participants started to stir in pots and pans. The other participants bent down on their knees and started to make fire — because you cannot cook without fire. This was a fine example of a cultural difference and prompted lots of laughter. It also showed us that these simple games are very helpful in addressing and explaining cultural differences.'

procedures, and rewards (Hogan, 2007.)

5.4 USING IMPROVISATION EXERCISES

When working in multicultural teams, it is important to map and
describe the differences between cultures. Using cultural values
can be a helpful tool. We describe some cultural values in the table
below. Using these topics helps to focus the dialogue and bring the
differences to light. Mapping and describing the cultural values is a
first step towards gaining a deeper insight into cultural differences,
beyond the stereotypes, and bridging those differences.

Individualism 'I' focus	**Collectivism** 'we,' 'group,' 'team' focus
Respect rules of behavior and protocol	**Casual politeness** informality
Hierarchy many levels in society, status, protocol	**Equality** few levels in society, equal treatment and access to resources
Indirect communication Diplomatic, circular, metaphor, analogies	**Direct communication** to the point, blunt
Experienced time flexible	**Clock time** on time, punctuality, deadlines

Table **Cultural values** (Hogan, 2007)

These cultural values can be an excellent start for a line-up exercise
(see toolbox page 130) in order to discuss the differences between
the cultures. To appreciate the difference between clock time and
experienced time, try the '1 minute excercise (page 82).

JAPAN FOR BEGINNERS

Gijs, Joost and Cyriel are members of the Applied Improvisation Network. There are regular conferences around the world. I (Joost) attended the Tokyo conference in 2009. This was the first time I encountered cultural differences in the improvisation world. Japan is a 'high context' and hierarchical society, with many protocols and unwritten rules. As a first time visitor, it was a puzzling and exciting experience. The conference started with a lesson on exchanging business cards. It appeared to be a protocolled way of offering, accepting and complimenting each other's business cards.

Shawn Kinley experienced the following in Japan, a good example of indirect communication: 'In various cultures, what is not said or done is sometimes the more important thing. I was teaching classes in Tokyo and my interpreter was showing me around the city. At one point he was a little lost and approached a stranger to enquire which direction we should take. The conversation took approximately 10 minutes and went something like this.

"Hello."

"Hello."

"It is a nice day for a walk."

"Yes, it is."

"There are many places to walk to, aren't there?"

"Yes, I am myself walking to a place."

"Yes, and many places are in locations that are not always so easy for people to find."

On and on it went as they circled around the definition of what we needed. The result was that we were still lost as it was assumed that the man might not know the location and therefore would probably not know the direction... In Japan, you wouldn't want to put someone in the position where they don't know something in public. They would 'lose face'.'

Experience this yourself with the 'Talk in Methaphors' exercise on page 168

CUSTOMER SERVICE

CHAPTER 6

Customer Service is the core of almost every business enterprise, yet the leaders of most companies don't view it or treat it that way. Instead of seeing customer service as an opportunity, they view it as a cost to be controlled. For most managers, this means scripts and a hard set of rules. The results are generally terrible for the customers and the employees alike.

What happens when Customer Service is imbued with improvisational skills and culture?

Good things happen!

6.1 WHAT IF WE COULD CHANGE THE WORLD?

Do you work in a company that provides Customer Service? If you work anywhere, I hope you said yes.

This chapter is specifically written for:

- Customer Service Managers
- Customer Service Representatives
- Executive Management
- Sales Management
- Salespeople
- People who work for companies who think they aren't responsible for Customer Service
- Consumers of Customer Service

We may be talking to everyone!

We all want the world to be a better place, but many of the problems seem overwhelming and hard to solve. I offer you one area where we can all work together make life much more pleasant.

Think about all of the bad experiences you've had on the phone, instant chatting or on the Internet with banks, insurance companies and technical support. How many of your days have been nearly ruined by these encounters where you not only didn't get what you needed, but you were left feeling unvalued or undervalued as a customer (much less as a human being)? Even when the transaction accomplishes what you needed, you are often left with anger, frustration or other negative feelings.

Customer Service can be done better. We don't have to have negative experiences every time we call or write. We can take better care of each other. And this is how we can change the world for good.

Improvisation can show us how to do this. And so can ice cream!

6.2 A VISIT TO THE ICE CREAM STORE

You can get ice cream in many different places, in many different forms and in many different flavors. In my hometown of Portland, Oregon, we've earned a reputation for "artisan-made" products and as a "foodie town". There are many special places to get extraordinary food.

One of my favorites is a small chain of stores called *Salt and Straw*. This local company makes and sells incredible ice cream with unusual flavors like Pear Bleu Cheese, Arbequina Olive Oil and Bone Marrow with Bourbon- Smoked Cherries. Portlanders stand in line at their stores for 30-60 minutes during the summer months. When you get to the front of the line, there's no pressure to hurry your decision. You are encouraged to try all the flavors. The people behind the counter want to hear your stories, like the time I remarked on their Mince-Meat Pie flavor – the woman serving me wanted to know the whole story: My mother made delicious Mince-Meat Pie at Thanksgiving and Christmas, but my friends would never even try it; they even made fun of me for liking "pie with meat in it" (the filling is made from fruits, spices and sugar and contains no meat). My server drew the story out of me and connected the dots to our current experience together. Then she gave me a scoop of incredibly delicious and meaningful ice cream.

I still remember that the ice cream was great, but my memory of how I was treated sticks with me.

> *"I've learned that people will forget what you said, people will forget what you did, but people will never forget how you made them feel."*
> *– Maya Angelou, Poet*

Even more interesting to me is the experience of repeated visits to

83

Salt and Straw. The experiences are always delightful, but they are all different. There's no script!

6.3 "BUT WE NEED SYSTEMS! WE CAN'T JUST MAKE IT UP!"

The thought of improvisation strikes panic in the hearts of management. Improvisation implies a lack of control, a lowering of management status (we'll talk about that in 6.4 and 6.5) and a potential separation anxiety ("They might not need my management expertise to function!") Due to management's fears, the response to new situations is usually expressed in new rules or new additions to a standard script.

Old visions of efficiency call for customers to be treated in exactly the same manner, and call for starting them from the same place. We need a script!

- A few customers call a computer support center without having plugged in their system or turned it on; now the script requires us to ask everyone if their system is powered on.
- We sometimes forget to "appreciate" our customers, so now the script tells us we must always say "we appreciate your business", sometimes over and over and over.
- One customer figures out how to take advantage of existing rules – **We need a new rule!**
- A telephone response system asks for an account ID number, and then the representative asks for the same information when they come on the line. We add requirements without considering the whole experience.

How many customer interactions really follow your script? How many days turn out exactly as you planned them? How many times do circumstances conspire to make your team short-handed? You are already improvising. You are already responding to changes and emergencies. Wouldn't it be helpful to respond more systematically?

84

In Chapter One, we learned that improvisation could be a means to support organizations and the professionals working in them. And here's the secret: improvisation is not simply making things up off the top of our head or "winging it". It exists within a framework. It's a system we can use when our traditional systems break down. It's also a system we should put in place as a set of consistent habits. It's a *highly refined system of observing, connecting and responding.*

Within that highly refined system, we find the following touch points:

- Listening – truly listening – by being present
- Accepting others and their circumstances, as well as accepting our own circumstances
- Supporting – making others look good
- Taking competent risks – stepping outside of the script when needed
- Letting go of mistakes – learning from mistakes, but not wallowing in them

Listening

In most Customer Service environments, **Listening** is glossed over in favor of finishing the transaction or phone call. In their hurry to move on, many people listen to only a quarter or a third of what the other person is saying. As soon as they think they have the subject matter, they prepare their response and shut down their listening skills.

Improvisors are trained to "listen like thieves". Thieves often commit crimes of opportunity – they set out to do one thing, and because another possibility occurs, they change direction and take advantage of it. They **didn't expect the opportunity, but they are open to it** if it happens. If performance improvisors don't listen with care, they will miss good opportunities as well as information important to their scene. A scene that starts out about one thing will often turn out to be about something quite different because the performers listened to what was happening and took advantage of it by taking the scene in a new and interesting direction.

86

Dr. Dave Russ is a Chiropractor. We were recently chatting about Customer Service, and he gave me the following examples:

Ask "Patient One" why they've come to the office and they might say, "My hip hurts."

"Patient Two" says, "Well, five years ago I had bunion surgery on my left foot. No, my right foot. Anyway, since then I haven't been able to wear any shoes except for open toed sandals. So last April I was in Nordstrom and I found this really cute pair of sandals, which I bought even though they weren't on sale. I loved them so much! But they had no traction on the sole. So I took them with me to Hawaii, where the first three days I stayed at the Hilton at Waikiki, which is nice but really crowded. Then we went to Kauai which is MUCH nicer, but a little more down-home, and the place we were staying was a bungalow, not that nice but right on the beach. The front stairs were a little slick from the rain the night before. So I had my coffee, KONA coffee...SO GOOD.... and as I was walking down the stairs I was sipping my coffee and not paying attention. I had on my sandals, with the slippery soles, and I didn't FALL fall, I just slipped and my left foot went forward like, an inch or two. Maybe more. I don't know, but I didn't actually fall. And now my hip hurts."

Patient One will require a little more investigation to get to the root of the problem.

If you have a busy medical practice, you might not be able to listen all the way through Patient Two's story, but it has a lot of value. A careful listener now knows how the injury was first noticed, some important background about prior conditions and some valuable insight into what matters to the patient.

In Customer Service, we often make presumptions about the problem, without listening for the clues the customer gives us about their goals. Ask informed questions and then listen. **Ask what the goal is, as opposed to what the problem is.** What is

87

really going on is rarely communicated immediately. It's how people are.

Focus on this customer at this moment. And listen with all of your energy.

Accepting

People don't always act in an efficient manner. At the beginning of our interactions, we don't know who they are, what their history might be or what problems they might be having.

In Chapter 5, we learned that even simple assumptions could cause complications when we don't understand the cultural underpinnings of someone's actions or words. We also don't know whether someone might be dealing with particular life burdens. If we are trained to **Accept** that people bring us value as customers, and are not a burden to us, we will be more inclined to provide them with a great experience, no matter how they approach us. Improvisation helps us respond to where people are at that moment.

We assume the best in our customers and co-workers. This allows us to connect more easily with them and to let them know that we are on their side.

Systems sometimes fail. Sometimes, we also have to accept the circumstances: we don't have enough staff, enough time, and enough information. If it's within our power, yes, of course we change things or fix the problem. If it's not, we choose to simply do our best.

An improvisational mindset allows us to make the best of whatever situation we are presented with. We don't waste energy and effort being upset if things don't go as planned, or if people don't behave in the expected manner. We "roll with it".

The result is less of a tendency to fight circumstances and more of a path to finding a solution that fits the situation.

Supporting

Improvisors love to **make other people look good**. It's one of the 7 Habits. We honor each other by listening carefully, staying in the moment with them, honoring their ideas, building on those ideas and trading leadership. This attitude, transplanted to a Customer Service situation, is incredibly valuable.

The most important times to support each other are when things go wrong or there's hard work to do. Improvisors like to say, "I've got your back" before they perform together. It's a way of expressing that we are connected, we're on the same team and we'll be there for each other.

In the business world, "I've got your back" means we're aware of what's happening around us; we understand what our teammates are there to do and we look for opportunities to make things go more easily.

As humans, it's sometimes easier to blame others – customers and co-workers – when things aren't going right. Compassion, on the other hand, is a beautiful thing. A high-functioning team uses compassion for each other to bolster performance.

Compassion means we expand "I've got your back" to include those times when everything doesn't go as planned – even when mistakes are made and co-workers "fail". When we are able to perform with others, without looking over our shoulders, and without thinking that the proverbial axe may fall at any time, we can focus our energy on getting the job done. We might also enjoy the job.

Without compassion, employees will "play defense". They won't work to accomplish the most; they will work to avoid mistakes.

Taking Competent Risks

Companies and their employees often "play it safe" to avoid making errors. This frequently means that "rules are rules" and the

89

policies behind them cannot be changed or even bent a little bit.

In most Customer Service settings, a mistake has already happened. It may be a product failure or a procedural error, or it might even be a mistake made by the customer. The mistake is causing the interaction to begin with. There are times when the established rulebook will take care of everything, but there are many times when it does not meet the needs of the particular situation. How do we move forward when everything we know doesn't help?

Here come three more of the improvisor's 7 Habits: **Experiment; Use Your Intuition;** and **Dare to Fail**.

New situations require new thinking and new solutions. Customer Service Representatives (CSRs) need the permission and freedom to **Take Competent Risks**. Stepping outside the lines can often solve problems in everyone's favor. Teaching CSRs to use their intuition and experience to create new or customized solutions wins customer loyalty, and probably serves to save time and money in most cases by shortening what could be a protracted battle.

The word "competent" is an important piece; nobody benefits from employees trying something without any reason to think it might work. Remember, we are not "winging it." It's not our job to simply end the phone call or interaction as quickly as possible. We want to end it well, for both parties.

The best solution to a problem is not solved by simply "giving away the store"; we want to balance the outcome. Finding this balance takes experience, and sometimes guidance. Throwing brand new employees into situation where you expect them to correctly analyze, improvise solutions and delight customers is taking an "incompetent" risk. Competent risks are based on experience, paired with flexibility.

Conversely, forcing all employees, particularly experienced ones, into exclusively sticking to scripts, will cost you customer goodwill, and eventually, will cost you sales as customers seek a better experience.

I switched internet providers 5 years ago, after I called a call center, explained my problem, and was forced to endure answering 13 questions from a script; the 13 questions had been answered in my opening statement. With a small amount of listening – not even true, focused listening, the CSR could have put the script down, saved time (and aggravation) and gotten me the help I needed. My two locations might still be using and paying for their services today. Instead, I get 4 pieces of mail a week from them, detailing their offers and bragging about their "great service", while I pay for service from a different provider.

Even with our best efforts, systems sometimes fail. That's what the next piece of the improv system is most needed.

Letting Go of Mistakes
Mistakes happen. As a customer, I find doing business is easy when everything goes according to plan. What's more interesting to me is what happens to our business relationship when someone makes a mistake.

The key to making mistakes work FOR us instead of AGAINST us is simple. **Note that a mistake has happened, correct it, share it with your team so it doesn't get repeated, and move on.** Spending time assigning blame, pointing fingers and over-reacting benefits no one. If we put energy into blame, we start encouraging people to cover mistakes up instead of "owning them". Think of a time when a cover-up wasn't far worse than the original transgression. I expect you'll be thinking for a long time before you come up with an example.

"Letting Go of Mistakes" can be open to misinterpretation. It's not an excuse to keep making the same mistakes over and over.

I'm a loyal customer, and I've had a credit card through a local bank since I was in high school. Recently, the bank was purchased

91

by BMO Harris Bank, who applied a few of their own rules to my account. One of my business vendors called me to report that a regular monthly payment had been declined; when I called BMO Harris, they told me that they "hold" payments I've made to the account for "5 business days" if the payments I've made total over $10,000.

I'll try to make this crystal clear: I had a $25,000 credit line, and I have never – not once – had a late payment. They were failing to credit payments to my account for 5 business days **AFTER they already had the money from my business checking account**. We are no longer transferring money via horse and carriage. It's not just that there was approval to get the money from my account; they already had the money.

A couple of months in a row with bills in the $15,000 range, and suddenly, I had a problem. When I called, they told me I was a "great" customer and unfroze the credit. I found out the next day (another vendor had a decline) that it "locked" again at midnight, and that I would have to call every day to "unlock it". Several supervisors told me that they could not make an exception to the general rule. They "understood" my frustration, but knew that the mistake their company was making was going to happen again and again.

One supervisor told me that the card I had "wasn't intended to be used" in the way I was using it. I was using it to pay for goods and services. BMO Harris Bank was correct in that their credit card was not the right card. I'm now happily using the card from a rival bank.

In our improv training, we focus on "sharing" mistakes. A miscue by one person is the responsibility of all of us. This helps us with our customers, too. We don't have to apologize for ourselves (which can be hard to do without sounding insincere in business situations), but we can apologize on behalf of the company. This is easier to do when we develop the habit of sharing mistakes. This also brings the responsibility to get rules that don't work changed.

92

You have to tell your managers about the problem.

The other side of mistakes, one that we love in the improvisational world, is that mistakes often lead us to new, and beneficial discoveries. Mistakes are better viewed as opportunities. BMO Harris Bank had an opportunity to improve my experience, and they chose not to take it.

When we:

- Listen
- Accept
- Support
- Take Competent Risks and
- Let Go of Mistakes;

we can promptly act on a customer's concern, fix the problem and create unexpected delight.

Improvisational tools are very useful, and your people can learn them in fun and rewarding workshops. One tool, however, holds the key to successful Customer Service.

6.4 STATUS

Improvisors use a number of tools to make their work meaningful and interesting. Narrative methods, mime, characterization and personal experience are examples of specific things we use to create scenes that audiences will want to watch. Status is a very powerful tool used to create forward motion and stakes in our scenes.

We see status used every day in the offstage world, too. Every exchange we have with another human being has some element of status playing a part. Parents have higher status than their children. The person who has something that someone else wants has higher status, simply based on possession. Kings and Queens, Prime Ministers and dictators have a high status conferred upon

93

them by society's traditions and laws. In most work situations, managers have a natural high status, while the people who work for them have lower status.

Onstage, status give improvisors the ability to move forward from the current situation, and that ability comes from a natural set of reactions to status:

- A high status person will usually act to preserve their status in relationship to a lower status person, by either raising their own status or taking action to lower the status of the other person.

- A low status person will usually attempt to change the status quo by taking action to raise their own status, or by attempting to pull down, or lower the status of the high status person.

Invariably, **status battles result in conflict**. In improvisational scenes, this can be both fascinating and hilarious to watch, as players maneuver and scheme to preserve or switch status.

In real life, these conflicts can result in destructive behavior. Think about a disagreement or fight that has occurred between your family members, or those of someone close to you. The root cause is almost always a simple battle for status.

The same situation happens in the work place. Disagreements between employees are usually based in status battles; fighting for a promotion, for notice from management, for credit for having a good idea. All of these involve a person or a group taking higher status for themselves and reducing the status of others.

One way to survive **status battles** is to recognize them as a game. You can play the game on someone else's terms, and get sucked into their battle, or you can play the game on your terms and subvert it for good.

94

First thing to mind

Yes And

Listen

People want to cooperate

...llowers
...er is tasty

...nga line

...bsened
...et coyotes
...mwork *z
...s not ~~Bad~~ Bad
...to be wrong
...ap

...to paint -twitter
...ty hard under pressure
...wait for perfect
...nts help
...outside box
...n
...l vs. verbal
...kinesthetic
...y cares

Yes And

Don't wait for perfection

Okay to be wrong

Listen

Nobody cares about you

Follow the follower

Constraints help

People want to cooperate

Don't
for p

I like
I wish
What if

What if everyone in your company understood that good Customer Service is made much easier to deliver when you learn about *matching status*?

6.5 STATUS IN CUSTOMER SERVICE

Every interaction between your company and your customers involves status.

When your customer calls (or comes into your business, or contacts you over the internet), they are usually having a problem with your product, service or the billing. Having a problem in the first place gives them lower status. They are seeking help from your customer service representative (this person could be anyone in your company), and the customer perceives that your company has the help or the solution they need. This naturally gives your representative higher status; they have something the customer wants.

In most traditional customer service interactions, a **status battle** ensues. The employee acts in a way that will help them maintain their status. They treat the incoming customer as less knowledgeable, as someone who can't use the product or service properly, or someone who quite naturally is unable to pay the bill in the manner that the company expects.

How many times have you called for computer tech support and the first question asked you is this:

"Is the equipment plugged in?"

In many cases, this is simply meant as a preventative toward wasting time, but the result, over 95% of the time, is a customer who thinks their time is being wasted and that they are being insulted. And what happens? The customer begins an attempt to raise their status and the battle is underway. Remember my Internet Service Provider with the 13 questions? I raised my status

96

by giving my business to another company.

Another interesting piece of this puzzle: most employees (particularly those in customer service call centers) do not feel that they have high status within their companies. This leads them to seize the high status they are given at the beginning of a call and defend it at all costs. Because employees seem so interested in maintaining what little high status they have, most interactions are structured to begin badly.

You have a choice. You can make these interactions about who wins and who loses – a *Status Battle* – or you can take a simple fact to heart:

> When we aim for even status, everyone is inspired to work together for the right solution.

Think of the best marriages – the best business partnerships – the best sports teams. What they have in common is that everyone involved is at equal status, or close to equal status (we'll talk more about shifting status in the Leadership section.) This holds true for our customer service interactions.

When our employees understand this dynamic, they can act to use it for good.

We've worked with for years with companies dealing with status in Customer Service, and we've discovered that trying to act with lower status than the customer doesn't work – it may be worse than acting with higher status. One thing to make clear with your employees is this: when they apologize to a customer, they do not have to be sorry themselves, which lowers their internal status. They are expressing an apology for the organization. The client needs to hear it, but it does not have to a personal apology.

Working to match the customer's status allows us to get things done by establishing empathy and trust. Expressing that you truly understand their problem gives us the basis to solve the problem.

It requires active listening and the practice of matching status. Relatively equal status allows both parties to take positive steps and exchange leadership in problem solving.

6.5 LEAD BY EMPOWERING YOUR PEOPLE

In improv performance scenes, leadership and status (who is in charge) change constantly. Based on the needs of the moment, leadership may shift between players as often as every sentence spoken, or even every gesture. Paul Sills, the great teacher, called this "Follow the Follower". Everything a performer does is a response to the other performers, instead of pushing a pre-conceived idea. When paired with the concept of leadership, matching status becomes "Follow the Follower".

In business, this means allowing your people to respond to what is happening with the customer *right now*. This may feel like taking a risk, because you are giving some of your leadership to your front line employees, but the best companies do this. It's not the old axiom of "the customer is always right." Customers aren't always right. It's a new, improvisational vision of "**the employee has the power to make the right decision, right now.**"

Scripts hold status in place. Let your employees explore matching status and you are empowering them to solve problems in a manner that delights customers, because it's a response to **what is actually happening now and what is needed now.** Delighted customers keep coming back to your company. *

Southwest Airlines continues to operate profitably and delight customers in US domestic air travel. Some of it is their focus on keeping things simple: they fly a fleet of Boeing 737 jets, so they don't have to stock different parts and have multiple training protocols. They also hedge their jet fuel purchases, to keep one of their highest expenses more predictable. What truly sets Southwest apart is their focus on their employees. They don't operate under a mantra of "the customer is always right". They empower their employees to do the right thing under the current circumstances. I've been exposed to how this works over and over; sometimes the decisions involve me directly, and many times, I've just watched as Southwest service reps and flight attendants made things better for passengers around me.

My company uses the services of a local printing company in Portland, Oregon, called GISI. I've taken photocopying, sign printing and other business to them for over 20 years. In that time, there have been 3 managers at the local outlet; this is in an industry where you're lucky to see the same person twice in a row. They've always been willing to do a little extra for us. Recently, when we changed branding and I was sending in files using new logo formats, GISI offered to check through my work to make sure everything would print to my satisfaction before I spent money on large format and color output. That prevented a couple of ugly errors on my part. Better than that is what happens when someone makes a mistake; in 20-plus years, I've never been dissatisfied with their response to a problem. They are always prompt, and never point fingers. Best of all, the front line workers and local outlet managers have never had to "check with corporate" to make things right. They just act. It's delightful! It's also efficient – for everyone involved.

Our company, CSz Portland, offers improv comedy shows to the public; we haven't missed a weekend since 1993! Each of our people is empowered to take care of our customers. We're always delighted to switch fans' seats to a show time that's better for them. The occasional mistake on our part is smoothed over with free beverages or free tickets to another show. There's only one problem: our customers routinely seem shocked that we are willing to be reasonable, friendly, prompt and honorable. They don't have that experience with many companies, and that is a shame.

6.6 HOW CAN YOU APPLY IMPROV TO CUSTOMER SERVICE?

If putting this to work in your organization were as simple as just

99

telling people to improvise, it would probably happen. It's not that simple, but it's also not terribly difficult.

- **Serve** everyone in your company as if they are your "customers"; and everyone needs to know they are all in Customer Service
- Get some **Applied Improvisation training** from an experienced professional
- **Communicate** what you discover throughout your company
- **Empower** your people to make the decisions they need to make
- **Measure** the right things, including customer satisfaction scores. Watch for complaint numbers to drop and reduced repeat calls from customers on the same problem. Call times are less important. Sometimes short calls are the result of customers giving up on your bad service.

Start by exposing your managers to Applied Improvisational training. In working with front line Customer Service people, the first question I'm usually asked is this: "When are you going to work with our managers?" The front line people see the value; they want their managers to buy in and then **empower them** to use the tools they've learned.

There are wonderful people all over the world who can lead your team to discoveries in improvisation. Start from the top, and empower your people. Think about the experience of ice cream. Customer delight will follow.

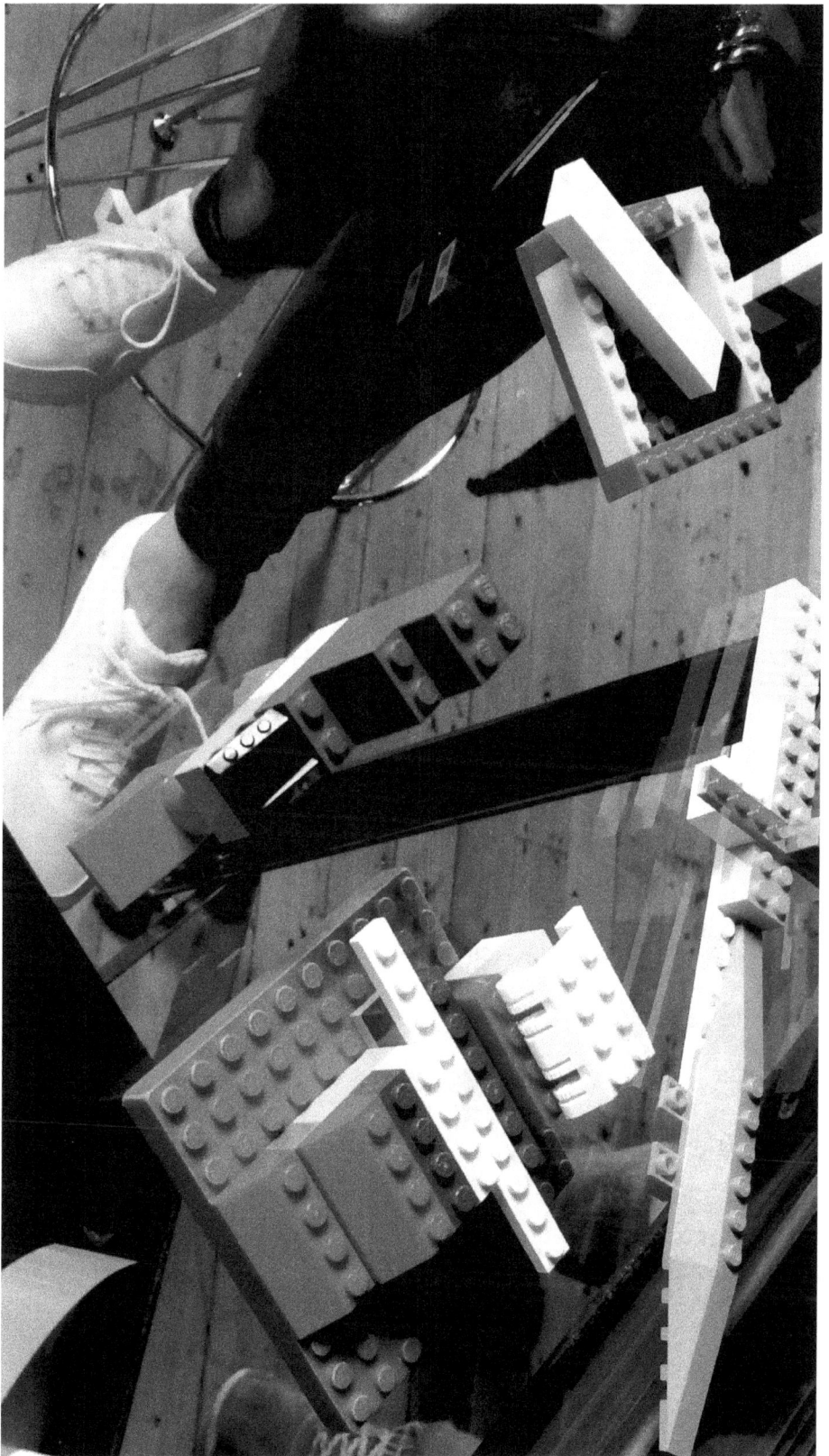

PART 3
TOOLBOX WITH EXERCISES

Now that we've discussed the theory of organizational improvisation and zoomed in on the professional skills, it's time to see how you can learn these skills. In part 3, we have an extensive list of exercises that you can use to train yourself and others in organizations. Coaches can use these exercises to boost their ability to teach the professional skills of improvisation.

The exercises are listed in alphabetical order. You can also use the table at the back of the book to search for the right exercise for a specific skill or habit. We've also divided the exercises according to what part of a session they are appropriate for. If you want to teach organizational improvisation in a workshop, some exercises are better suited for the beginning of the workshop and others are better suited to end with.

For this book, we have asked some of our most esteemed colleagues to share their favorite exercises with you. These colleagues come from all over the world, from The Netherlands and Belgium (our own countries), to America, Asia, Africa, and Australia. Please feel free to contact any of our colleagues if you wish them to train you or your organization in the ways of improvisation. Their contact details and geographical origin are on the world map which you can also find at the back of the book.

1 MINUTE EXERCISE

Objective creating a relaxed atmosphere where the audience can 'be present'
Summary the audience has to estimate 1 minute of clock time
Duration 2 minutes
Number of participants unlimited

Description of the activity

Ask everybody to stand up. Explain that the participants have to estimate one minute of clock time in silence. The challenge is that they can't count numbers so they have to 'experience' the duration of a minute. When you feel that one minute has passed then you can open your eyes again and sit down (very silently). Count down from three, and at zero the minute starts. Make sure that you have a stopwatch ready. You will notice that the first person will sit down after 30 seconds and there's a good chance that some people will still be standing after two minutes. After two minutes you stop the exercise and tell how much time it took for the first person to sit down, and the last person. This shows that it is quite hard to be conscious of the clock time (without counting or our clocks) and it helps to let people arrive into the 'present.'

1-2-3 CLAP-
STAMP-SCRATCH

Objective warm-up exercise, to break thinking patterns
Summary in pairs, you build up a pattern which is subsequently broken by replacing the spoken words in the pattern with physical actions
Duration at least 10 minutes
Number of participants unlimited (the exercise is done in pairs)

Description of the activity

Pair up with a partner and stand opposite each other. In your pair, count to three together. Person A starts counting on 'one', person B shouts 'two' and then back to A for 'three', after which B starts counting all over again from 'one.' Do this for a while until you have a nice rhythm going. Once this has happened, everyone has to replace the word 'one' with a clap; i.e. 'one' is no longer spoken, but instead clap your hands once. The words 'two' and 'three' are still spoken. Continue doing this until everyone is, once again, familiar with the pattern, and then replace the word 'two' with a stamp of the foot. So, 'one' is a clap, 'two' a stamp of the foot and, for the time being, the word 'three' is still spoken. Once everyone has got the hang of this pattern, the final step is to replace the word 'three' with a scratch of the head. Everyone has now stopped counting altogether; instead, there are only physical actions left in the pattern.

Tips & directions
- Increase the tempo as soon as people have got the hang of a particular rhythm.
- Explain this exercise by placing it in the context of breaking thinking patterns. When you want to come up with new ideas, you will also have to break certain patterns and this is a great practical exercise to illustrate this.

AN ALIEN HAS LANDED...

Objective to connect with a total stranger
Summary getting somebody to move without speech
Duration 10–15 minutes
Number of Participants small groups or trios

Description of the activity

Ask one participant to lie down on the floor. Explain to the group that an alien has landed and that we do not know how to connect with this alien. We don't know whether he or she is dangerous or not. Our first task as a group is to get in touch with the alien, to find out how we can communicate with him or her. We have to try to get the alien seated on a chair.

In the debrief the trainer can ask what works and what doesn't. Ask the alien why he/she responded to certain actions. What made him/her move?

Tips & directions

• As the trainer, you can give the alien some instructions before he lies down. E.g.: do not react to physical contact, copy all the movements and sounds of the other, react only to one specific word or action.
• For the participants, it is important to try as many avenues as possible to discover how to get in touch with the alien. They have to explore different ways in order to find the right way.
• For the alien, it is important to let him or herself be convinced by the participants by things that he or she likes. The objective is not to stay on the floor at all costs.
• You can do this exercise in small groups or in trios, where there is one alien, one participant and one observer.

CHARACTER CREATION

➔ *Kat Koppett's favorite exercise*

Objective collectively creating characters
Summary as a group, the participants create a character, one feature or personality trait at a time. Beginning with a name, participants randomly take turns making offers until the character feels complete, or the group loses a clear image of it.
Duration 10–20 minutes
Number of participants 2–20 per circle

Description of the activity
Have the participants sit in a circle.
Provide (or ask the group for) a fictional first and last name of a character. (e.g. Sally McMurphy, Renaldo Hernandez, Clyde Clump, Isadora Ilandavalle.)
Have the participants randomly offer characteristics, building on the offers of others. (e.g. "Sally McMurphy" is a waitress." "She has huge green eyes." "She came to America from Ireland two years ago." "She came because her family was really poor and she wanted to seek her fortune.")

If someone in the group loses the picture of the character, because he feels an offer contradicts something that has already been said, or that it just doesn't make sense, he can say, "I can't see it." Then, the group begins again with a new character name.

End work on a character when the group can no longer see it or feels the description is complete.
Play as many rounds as you wish.

Variations
- Describe an environment. (e.g. a hotel room, a haunted house, a train station, an office, a barn.)
- Describe a fictional product. (e.g. Wiggy Wash, Yum-yum Paste, Ever-clean, Box-in-a-box.)
- Describe a character beginning with a characteristic other than a name. (e.g. a profession, an age, a nationality, a physical characteristic.)
- Describe the future state of the team.

Tips & directions
- In the beginning, encourage the group to speak up when they lose sight of the character. This allows the group to assess the kinds of risks they are willing to take and take a look at their assumptions.
- Use as an exercise on accepting offers. As the exercise progresses, encourage the participants to expand their ability to "see" characteristics that they were rejecting at first.
- Encourage the group to take their time.
- If a few members are dominating, ask for input from those who have not yet offered suggestions. Going around the circle in order can provide equal opportunity for members to partcipipate, but removes the possibility of debriefing about participation and control

Source *Adapted from Keith Johnstone*

CIRCLE OF EMOTIONS

Objective teamwork, observation, association
Summary to copy an emotion and make it bigger
Duration 10 minutes
Number of participants groups of 15 people

Description of the activity

This is an alternate version of the Circle of Sound exercise.
In this instance, the participants pass on an emotion. Someone
starts off by making an expression and a sound which match a
certain emotion. This is then passed along the circle. At the end,
ask the person who started off the exercise which emotion he
had in mind.

Variations

This exercise lends itself to endless variations:
• Allow the emotion to grow bigger and bigger as it goes around
  the circle. The person who starts off the exercise must make the
  emotion as small as possible. The last person in the circle has to
  make the emotion as big as possible.
• Allow the emotion to go from small to big and back to small again.

Tips & directions

• If the emotion is growing bigger, the instructor has to monitor
  the build-up carefully. The emotion should not be at its biggest
  halfway through the circle because otherwise there is no way
  anyone who is next can make it any bigger. This exercise also
  shows whether a group is capable of working together and moving
  beyond (their own) boundaries.
• As the instructor, you decide the starting point and direction
  within the circle. By doing so, you automatically determine who
  will go last and has to go completely crazy...

112

CIRCLE OF EYE CONTACT

Objective nonverbal communication, concentration
Summary reacting to eye contact
Duration 20 minutes
Number of participants groups of 10–15 people

Description of the activity
All the participants stand in a circle. Person A starts off the
exercise by seeking eye contact with another participant,
person B. As soon as A has managed to make eye contact,
B nods and A starts to walk over to B's spot. B, in turn,
has to make sure that he can make eye contact with and
receives a nod from someone else (person C) before A arrives
at his spot. And so on. In case of bigger or more advanced
groups, several people can do the exercise at once.

Tips & directions
• Walk very slowly at first.
• Be very strict about the fact that a nod has to be given by the
  'receiver' first before the other person can start to walk over.
• Clearly indicate that the focus is on the person seeking eye
  contact instead of the person walking over. The other participants have to constantly look around to see if anyone is
  seeking eye contact with them.

CIRCLE OF SOUND

Objective teamwork, observation, association
Summary to copy a movement and sound
Duration 10 minutes
Number of participants groups of 15 people

Description of the activity
Everyone stands in a big circle. One person starts off by passing on a movement and sound to his right-hand neighbor. This person immediately passes on the same movement and sound to his neighbor. In this way, the movement travels around the circle. When the movement has gone around the whole circle once, every participant may make a change to it (amplifying or toning down the movement and sound or simply making a minor change.)

Tips & directions
Make sure that the participants do not start messing around from the start and changing the movement and/or sound straightaway. The idea is that they accept and copy an offer (in this case a movement and sound). There are endless variations to this exercise.

Variations
Pass on a movement and a sound to a random person who then passes on a completely different movement and sound to someone else. This exercise is all about speed. Encourage people to also alternate big movements and sounds with very modest ones.

CITY SOUND-SCAPE

Objective to accept, to work together towards a shared goal, flexible association

Summary the participants portray — through sound only — a city on a normal weekday

Duration at least 10 minutes

Number of participants 5–25

Description of the activity

Everyone stands closely together in a circle. Those who want to may close their eyes. Ask the participants to mimic the sounds of a city. Start off at nighttime when it is still very quiet. Then, the city gradually comes to life until it goes to sleep again at night.

Tips & directions

• Ask people to make sounds rather than use words.
• Every so often, you could shout out the time of day so that the participants know what type of sounds might occur at that time.

Variations

Instead of asking the participants to bring a city to life, ask them to create a zoo soundscape which would result in all sorts of different animal noises being produced.

CLUMPS

⊕ Alieke van der Wijk's favorite exercise

Objective networking exercise, warming up
Summary form groups based on all kinds of criteria
Duration 10 minutes
Number of participants unlimited (you need some open space)

Description of the activity
Ask people to form groups based on several criteria. These criteria could be physical elements or invisible elements or even opinions:
- form groups of 3 noses, 5 feet, 11 fingers
- hair length
- shoe size
- shirt color
- favorite movie genre
- holiday destinations
- years of experience in the company
- expectations of the workshop

YES AND... YOUR BUSINESS

COLOR/ADVANCE

Objective telling a story
Summary one person tells a story, another person helps him by saying 'color' or 'advance'
Duration 10 minutes
Number of participants Pairs

Description of the activity

The participants divide in pairs and choose who is A and who is B. A begins by telling a story. This is a true story or a well-known story such as a fairy tale. More advanced participants can make up a story on the spot. B helps A to keep the story interesting by saying 'color', in which case A gives more details about what is happening right now. A can describe emotions, the surroundings or some background about the characters. B can also say 'advance' to move along the story. A can describe the next action in the story. When the story is done, A and B switch roles.

Source Kat Koppett, adapted form Viola Spolin

COME HERE, COME HERE, GET OUTTA HERE

⊕ *Henk van der Steen's favorite exercise*

Objective networking exercise, warming up
Summary form groups based on all kinds of criteria
Duration 10 minutes
Number of participants unlimited

Description of the activity
This exercise can be used as a follow-up to 'Clumps'.
Have the participants divide themselves into groups of six.
The facilitator asks some questions, which the groups have
to answer. E.g.:
- Who has the longest tenure in the organization?
- Who has the most...(diplomas, CDs, etc.)
- Who has the largest/biggest/smallest...

After conferring and determining who that is, that person
shouts "I'm outta here!" and goes looking for another group.
The groups will now try to lure these people in by calling
'Come here, come here', until the group has the same amount
of people it started with. After this, the facilitator asks the
next question. Note that the groups should actively welcome
newcomers and strangers in their midst by asking 'Come here,
come here'.

Source *Andrew Welch*

COMMITMENT WALK

Objective to generate commitment so that people work towards the development/implementation of an idea
Summary indicate through physical distance whether you feel committed to the realization of a concept
Duration at least 10 minutes
Number of participants unlimited

Description of the activity

One person indicates that he wants to develop a particular concept further. This is the problem owner. The other people stand at a certain distance from the problem owner. By asking questions about the action plan for the concrete development of the concept, people can move closer or further away from the problem owner. Consequently, the action plan is concretized and the problem owner gets an idea of the level of commitment from the other participants. By adjusting certain aspects of the action plan, this level of commitment can be increased or decreased.

Tips & directions

It is not necessary for every participant to commit himself to a solution. The participants who have to work with the solution are the most important.

COUNT-UP

Objective to get a sense of each other, nonverbal communication
Summary count to 10 without making agreements
Duration at least 10 minutes
Number of participants groups of 10 people

Description of the activity

Stand in a circle and explain the rules of the game. The idea is to count from one to ten as a group but no agreements or patterns should be made as to who calls out a number when. You can't call out two numbers in a row (after you call out a number, at least one other person has to call out a number before you can go again). If two people call out a number at the same time, you have to start counting again from one. It is best to do this exercise with eyes closed or to ask the participants to focus on a particular point in the middle of the circle.

Tips & directions

- Someone who does not say anything is contributing just as much as someone who has called out three numbers.
- At first, you will find that you have to start counting all over again a lot because the participants call out a number at the same time. In this case, tell them that a calmer approach will possibly result in the group becoming better attuned to each other.
- If things are going really well, you can move on to counting to 20 or call out the letters in the alphabet.

DIAMOND DANCE/ DANCE IN LINE

Objective dance as a group by constantly switching leaders
Summary the entire group dances according to the moves made by constantly switching leaders
Duration 10–15 minutes
Number of participants 10 or more

Description of the activity

The facilitator designates multiple people as the leader. These can either be entire rows (first row, last row and people at the far sides of the group) or people at the corners of the group. One of these groups will start the dancing. The people behind them will mimic the moves they make. The people behind them will mimic their moves, and so on, until everybody is dancing. At some point, either at the initiative of the facilitator or the leaders, leadership switches. If the first row were the leaders, it changes to people standing at the far left of the group. After this it will switch to the last row and people on the far left.

Tips & directions

This is best done with an outgoing group of people, or after another dancing exercise. It can be a great way to sneak some learning into an evening program.

DOLPHIN TRAINING

Objective experience the subtle collaboration between leader and follower
Summary make another person do something without using words, just using sounds
Duration 20-30 minutes
Number of participants 20

Description of the activity

Let the participants sit in a half circle, or in the audience. Ask for one volunteer. Ask him to leave the room and when he is called back in the room, he has to perform a task. He will be guided by the audience. Ask the remaining participants to come up with a simple task, to be performed by the volunteer. E.g.: to touch his hair, to sit on a specific chair, etc. Ask the volunteer to enter the room. The audience has to command the volunteer with beeping sounds in order to let him complete his task. The more the volunteer reaches his goal, the higher and louder the beeping sound has to be.

Repeat this with another volunteer.

Then form pairs and let them try this themselves for 5 -10 minutes. Ask them to switch roles halfway.

Tips & directions

The essence of this exercise is to experience as leader how you can guide someone. When someone does not succeed in his task, who is to blame? The leader or the follower? How clear are the instructions, how clear is the goal? How good can you listen and react on each other?

122

DRAWING IN PAIRS

Objective acceptance, suspension of judgment, teamwork

Summary drawing a picture together without making agreements about what you are going to draw

Duration 10 minutes

Number of participants unlimited (the exercise is done in pairs)

Description of the activity

Every pair is given a piece of paper and two pens. Per pair, partners take turns to draw a certain line or shape on the piece of paper without either of them knowing what they are going to draw. So, they are drawing a joint picture without talking. Ask them to name the picture (written in the same way as the picture was drawn, i.e. without talking to each other and by each partner taking a turn to write a letter).

EVOLUTION

Objective warming up, fun, high energy
Summary the participants are challenging each other
with the rock-paper-scissors game to evolve from egg
to chicken to dinosaur to human being
Duration minimum 15 minutes
Number of participants unlimited

Description of the activity
Have the group in a circle. Everyone starts out as an egg
and clasps their hands above their head so that they
look like an egg. When you say "go", each person will
find another egg. Once they have found that person,
they will then farkle (rock, paper, scissors.) The loser
stays an egg and the winner becomes a chicken, holding
their arms like wings and making clucking noises. The
chicken then looks for another chicken while the egg
looks for another egg. When a chicken wins, it becomes
a dinosaur. Dinosaurs hold their hands out and roar.
If a chicken loses, it drops back down to an egg. Dinosaurs then find other dinosaurs, where they will play to
become the Ultimate People. Ultimate People put their
hands over their heads like Superman and look for others
like them. If a dinosaur loses, it goes back to being
a chicken, looking for other chickens. If an Ultimate
Person loses to another Ultimate Person, they go back
to being a dinosaur, and if they win, they stay Ultimate
People.

124

EXPERIENCE RING

→ *Frans Bosch' favorite exercise*

Objective realizing that organizational change is a collective process
Summary first the leader of a group tries to categorize the entire group, then the group is allowed to help.
Duration 10 minutes
Number of participants groups larger than 20 people

Description of the activity
Form a circle and ask people to think of the date they entered the company. Give the CEO, or other leader of the group, the assignment to put the group in order, from who has worked at the company the longest, to the one who arrived most recently. The CEO can ask questions and tell people where to stand in the circle, but the participants. He has two minutes to complete the exercise.

Of course, this is nearly impossible. "We're sorry, Mr. CEO, we asked you to do the impossible. Now let's do it again." This time, everybody can get involved. Talking is allowed and even beneficial. This probably will work.

Tips & directions
The moral of the story is to involve everybody. This is not only a lesson for the CEO, but also for the employees: take initiative by yourself, don't let the boss do all the work.

EXPLORING STATUS

Objective exploring different variations in status
Summary players make short scenes with different types
of status
Duration 20–30 minutes
Number of participants 3–4 players, audience and a facilitator

Description of the activity
In order to explore and deepen the concept of status, the
trainer asks two people to play a short scene with a clear
difference in status. E.g. an employee has to ask for a day
off with his boss.

The scene should be short and simple and is played in different
variations:
• The first round, the trainer gives the high status to the boss
  and the low status to the employee.
• The second round, the trainer gives the high status to the
  employee and the low status to the boss.
• The third round, the status is not decided on beforehand,
  but is allowed to emerge from the scene.

After the third round, the trainer asks the audience which actor
had the higher status, and which actor had the lower status.
Discuss it with the group if necessary.
The audience and the players might discover a difference in
formal status (in rank or hierarchy) and informal status, (in
body language.)

The trainer then asks them to play the same scene and tells the
actors to be 'in control' of the scene. Afterwards, the audience
decides who was most in control. Discuss it with the group if
necessary.

Another version is to ask the participants to be the most self-confident in the scene. Afterwards the audience decides who was the most self-confident. Discuss it with the group if necessary.

Tips & directions
- The scenes should be simple and the participants have to have some experience. It is not about the quality of the acting, but to experience and view the different ways of looking at high and low status.
- Another version can be to ask the players to be the most charismatic.

Source Alex Lamb, AIN 2010, Amsterdam

FACTS AND ASSUMPTIONS

Objective to experience the difference between facts and interpretation
Summary the group will look at someone and quickly mix facts with assumptions
Duration 15–20 minutes
Number of participants unlimited group

Description of the activity

The trainer stands before the group and asks: what do you see? The group members have to state only their **factual** observations. E.g.:.

- You're wearing a ring on your finger
- You have blond hair
- You wear glasses

Some of the observations are **assumptions**. The trainer has to make the difference between the two!

- You are married (assumption)
- You are handsome (opinion)
- You have bad eyesight (assumption)

At the end the trainer discusses the differences between facts and assumptions.

Tips & directions

You can do this exercise in pairs, but make sure that it is not a problem with the group to describe another person. If gender is a sensitive issue, pair with the same gender.

Variations

You can also ask the group to imagine the other person's life. E.g.: what kind of work does he do? What kind of house does he live in? What does his partner look like? This can be a good

Another version is to work with emotions. As a trainer you can enter the room with a certain emotional expression, without using words. Ask the group what they see (facts) and what they think is happening (assumptions).

FAINT & SUPPORT

Objective building trust between participants
Summary while walking around, some participants will 'faint'
and they will be saved by other participants
Duration 15–20 minutes
Number of participants unlimited (at least 20 participants)

Description of the activity
Form groups of 7 people (can be bigger or smaller depending
on the number of participants, but you should be able to form
at least 5 sub-groups.) Every group member gets a number
between 1 and 7. Then, ask the participants to walk around
randomly in the room (make sure that all the subgroups mix.)
Then explain that you are going to shout a number between
1 and 7 and that person will faint (of course, they should fake
fainting and make a short noise before falling.) The other
participants are responsible for 'saving' the people with that
number by supporting them and helping them get back on
their feet.

Tips & directions
- Start very slowly and shout one number at a time (at least
  in the beginning; after a while you can shout two or three
  numbers at the same time).
- To end this game, you can shout all the numbers at the same
  time and everybody will 'fall' on the ground.

130

FAMILY PORTRAITS

Objective warming up, fun, high energy
Summary the participants are going to 'build' a family portrait
Duration at least 10 minutes
Number of participants 7 or 8 participants (the rest can watch)

Description of the activity

This is a fun game to get everyone to work together.
Ask 7 or 8 participants to 'build' family portraits by posing as if they were in a picture.
E.g.: ask for a:

• Family of accountants, bean counters
• Family of fat or skinny people
• Family of pop stars
• Family of snakes, rats, cats
• Family of garden tools

Tell the participants you want to see who's who in the family. Once they get the exercise, make it a bit more difficult by asking to see who gets along with who, who's the black sheep of the family, and so on. It's a good exercise where participants have to watch each other closely.

FIND THE CHANGE

➔ *Nicole van der Ouw's favorite exercise*

Objective getting out of your comfort zone in change processes
Summary people have to change more and more parts of their appearances
Duration 15–20 minutes
Number of participants in pairs

Description of the activity

After dividing the group into pairs, tell the participants this is an exercise about reacting to changes and ask them to share their experiences freely. The exercise has three steps. Here are the instructions.

Step 1

- Carefully look at each other, so you know what they look like.
- Turn around so you don't see each other and change 5 things about your appearance.
- Turn back and try to guess which things your partner changed.

People will generally change small things and stay within their comfort zone.

Step 2

- Tell the participants the change was not enough to achieve the desired effect.
- Turn around and change 10 extra things.
- Turn back and try to guess which things your partner changed.

At this point, people will go a bit out of their comfort zone. They might start reacting to the exercise or trying to cheat. Let this happen and observe.

Step 3
- Tell the participants we are in a crisis and much more change is necessary.
- Turn around and change an additional 25 things which you haven't changed before.
- Turn back and try to guess which things your partner changed.

Here people will begin to rebel, saying it is impossible, or people will find extraordinary creativity, form alliances and so on.

Finally, tell people they change their appearance back if they want to. Sit down and discuss what people felt and what they observed.

Tips & directions
Observing what happens is crucial in this exercise. With large groups, try to have multiple facilitators or ask certain participants to act as observers.
As a last question, you can ask whether people kept any changes they made to their appearance.

FINGER APPLAUSE

Objective asking for applause in a funny way
Summary the audience starts to applaud starting with one finger
Duration 3 minutes
Number of participants unlimited

Description of the exercise
Have the audience clap not their hands, but start with one finger.
Then gently add more fingers until the whole hand is used.

Variations
Try having folks clap hands with their neighbors. Left hands up,
right hands down, so every person claps his right hand into his
neighbor's left hand and vice versa. Say 'hagawaga' when you
raise your right hand.

FLOWERPOTS

Objective to enrich ideas
Summary enriching ideas by calling out suggestions based on other ideas
Duration minimum 10 minutes
Number of participants 2 to 4 participants — the rest are the audience

Description of the activity

Two to four participants act out a certain solution. During the scene, the audience can call out ideas (based on previously compiled ideas) which the actors subsequently have to integrate into their scene. As a result, the solution is enriched with other ideas.

Tips & directions

This is quite a difficult exercise so make sure that not too many suggestions are being called out. It is also easier if the ideas which are being introduced into the scene can be integrated one way or another into the solution the actors have taken as their starting point.

FREE FALL

Objective to trust in the group as a whole,
Summary one participant in the middle of a circle formed by
the other participants lets himself fall and be caught by them,
in order to generate trust
Duration 20–30 minutes
Number of participants groups of 10 people

Description of the activity

Eight to ten participants form a circle around one person.
The person in the middle closes his eyes and holds his body
stiff (you could instruct this person to hold himself as stiff as
a board.) Next, he lets himself fall forwards and sideways. The
others catch him and can tell him which direction he should fall
in next. Start off by doing this exercise very gently! Also, make
sure people stand close enough to the person in the middle.

Tips & directions

• This is a 'scary' exercise for the person in the middle. Make
  sure that the participants have formed a solid circle before
  they catch someone.
• Any heavier participants should be caught by at least two
  people.
• When working with big groups, it is time-consuming to let
  everyone have a turn. In this case, you could do the exercise
  in pairs. One person lets himself fall backwards and the
  person standing behind him catches him. It is important that
  everyone gets to experience this exercise. When working in
  pairs, make sure that the partners in the pairs are of a similar
  strength.

GEOGRAPHICAL MAP

Objective to get to know each other based on geographical characteristics
Summary getting to know each other based on geographical characteristics
Duration 10–20 minutes
Number of participants unlimited

Description of the activity
Divide the performance area into the four points of the compass. The area represents the map of the region or country of your location. Also point out where the major cities are located. Then ask the participants to go stand in the spot that marks their place of birth. Once everyone has found their place, allow the people standing near each other to spend a few minutes getting to know each other.

Here, too, you could come up with lots of different versions. Where:
• do you work?
• did you go on holiday
  (in this case, turn the performance area into a 'world map')?
• do you live at the moment?
• did you go to university/school?
• would you never ever want to live?

Tips & directions
Make sure that everyone gets their turn. Remember to give some attention to those people who were born in exotic places and are standing on their own.

Variations
- When working with local groups, the map can be smaller (province, city, etcetera).
- When working with international groups, the map will have to be bigger.

GIBBERISH STORY

Objective nonverbal communication, suspension of judgment
Summary conduct a conversation in a made-up language
Duration 10 to 15 minutes
Number of participants unlimited (the exercise is done in pairs)

Description of the activity
This exercise, talking gibberish - or jabber talk - is about having
a conversation in a language that does not exist. You get to
make up certain sounds and fictitious words. In pairs, tell each
other a story in gibberish about something you have recently
done or something that has recently happened to you. The
other person also responds in gibberish based on the sounds
and actions made by his partner. By doing this, you take away
the meaning of words and the intonation, volume and emotion
of the words become more important.

Tips & directions
- One way of letting people get used to talking gibberish is
  to tell them to have a conversation in a language they do
  not speak (for instance, Chinese or Russian). Most people
  are able to mimic sounds from a language they do not know.
- Ask the participants to act out an everyday activity in
  gibberish (for instance, buying a loaf of bread at the baker's
  or something related to work).

GCD: GREATEST COMMON DENOMINATOR

Objective to get to know each other based on shared characteristics
Summary exchange of personal information
Duration 15–20 minutes
Number of participants unlimited (the exercise is done in small groups)

Description of the activity
Divide the participants into small groups of three to four people. People within each small group have to exchange personal information with each other (where they live, number of children, hobbies, whatever.) The aim is to find a minimum of two characteristics which apply to every member in their group, preferably as concrete as possible (everyone plays badminton is more concrete than everyone plays a sport).

Tips & directions
Start off with a small group of three and then suddenly add a fourth person so that they have to start the exercise again. After a short while, divide people into new groups.

Variations
1. Turn it into a competitive game, try to find as many similarities per small group as possible.
2. Set themes around which groups can be formed. For instance: everyone who loves sports, move to the left, and everyone who hates sports, move to the right.

GREETING PEOPLE

Objective to get to know each other through various greetings
Summary greeting participants in different ways while walking around in the room
Duration 15–20 minutes
Number of participants unlimited

Description of the activity
Ask people to walk around the room and greet each other.
The first time, greet in the Western way by shaking hands.
After that, the possibilities are endless:
- an Indian greeting
- a Russian greeting
- in the style of old friends
- someone you do not trust
- someone with whom you share a secret connection
- cool guys/chicks from the Bronx
- someone you really hate
- cowboys
- aliens

Tips & directions
Build up the alternatives from little physical contact to more physical contact.

Variations
In this exercise, you can also play around with different moods (happy, angry, frightened, enthusiastic.)

HELPING BY SERVING

Objective Practicing servant leadership, building trust
Summary One person acts out a complex task, while another person tries to make this task as easy possible.
Duration 15 minutes
Number of participants A minimum of 2 persons

Description of the activity
Two (or more) participants will play out two scenes. In the first scene one person does a complex task and the other person gives directions from the sideline. In the second scene the second person tries to make the task as easy as possible by asking supportive questions and facilitating the task; handing the first person crucial items, moving stuff out of the way, etc.

Tips & directions
Complexity in a task can be simulated by giving contradicting assignments, such as: make a toy that embodies violence, but teaches a child a peaceful lesson.

HOT SPOT

Objective warm-up exercise, getting to know each other
Summary one person in the middle of a circle who starts to tell a story and when somebody else recognizes a 'topic', he jumps in and continues the story
Duration at least 10 minutes
Number of participants circles of at most 12 people

Description of the activity

Everyone stands in a circle. One person steps into the circle and starts to share some details about his personal life. At the moment that another person hears something that sounds similar to his own personal life, he takes over the story (by stepping into the middle) and tells something about his personal life. E.g.: "I'm Cyriel and I love to go on holidays to New Zealand..." If there's somebody else who also likes New Zealand, that person takes over and continues the story or can go in a different direction: "...I have two dogs and one cat..." and that person continues until somebody else recognizes something from his personal life.

Tips & directions

- Increase the tempo as soon as people know what they have to do.
- Explain that it is also about helping each other. So when a person is standing in the middle and is unable to come up with something, jump in and say that you sometimes also don't know what to say and give some other details.

HYPEMAN

Objective supporting each other
Summary the reporter asks the frontman a question, and the hypeman exaggerates his answer positively
Duration 10–15 minutes
Number of participants groups of three

Description of the activity
Divide the participants into groups of three. Each group of three chooses which of them will be the reporter, the frontman, and the hypeman. The reporter asks the frontman the following question: "Could you name one of your qualities?" The frontman gives an answer, e.g. "I'm friendly," upon which the hypeman starts to support the frontman by praising and positively exaggerating the frontman's quality. E.g.: "Friendly, friendly? He's so friendly, Mother Theresa used to call him for advice." Switch roles until everybody has played all the roles.

Tips & directions
You can debrief after the first or second change in roles, to see if the people notice a difference after they know what the exercise is about. This exercise is easy for people to do, because it is very verbal. It raises the energy level of a group enormously.

Source Matt Weinstein

INTELLIGENT CLAY

● *Belina Raffy's favorite exercise*

Objective creating profound insights into the dynamics of a situation you would like to transform and the interplay between key elements

Summary getting a group to help someone explore the current and desired future state of a situation and the dynamics involved between the key pieces

Duration 10–15 minutes

Number of participants groups of 1 director/sculptor plus 5 - 7 people

Description of the activity

A person takes the 'director/sculptor' role and chooses key elements and/or people in a situation that he would like to explore. Each element gets a large, legible sticky label. The director choses who from the group plays what role and gives out the labels. No one is allowed to play themselves. The director sculpts first the 'now' static state - getting the players to show relationships by body position, proximity, connection as is meaningful to the director. Once the frozen picture is complete and the participants know how it goes, the director then takes the players to a position across the room and sculpts the desired future state. Once this is set, players go back the first position and when told 'go' in silence move/morph so that they get from the 'now' position to the 'future' position. Once the players are finished in the 'future' position, they are held there as the director, then each player in turn, talks about what they noticed and what needed to happen for the future state to occur.

Tips & directions
In setting up the sculptures, each player will hear and feel dynamics of their role and interaction from the director. Encourage the players not just to walk from one state to another - but to imagine and act out what the dynamics between the roles need to be to create the desired future state. Best to run this activity after some body/movement work has been done.

Source *Brian Woodward, Colin Funk and others*

JOINT CLAP

Objective create a group sense
Summary doing a joint clap with your neighbors
in a rhythm
Duration 3–5 minutes
Number of participants unlimited

Description

Standing or sitting in a circle, ask participants to place
their right hand above their neighbor's left hand and
their left hand under their other neighbor's right hand.
Then the facilitator starts a rhythm where you clap the
hands together (so you clap with your neighbor.) After
one clap, you switch places (so the upper right hand
becomes the bottom right hand and the bottom left
hand becomes the upper left hand) and clap again
with your neighbor. The third clap is a regular clap
with both your own hands (not with your neighbors.)
Then you go to step one again.

Tips and directions

- Do it very slowly in the beginning and be part of the
  circle as the facilitator.
- Speed up when participants get into the rhythm.

148

JOLLY JOSEPH

Objective to learn names quickly
Summary participants make up an alliteration using their first name
Duration 10–15 minutes
Number of participants unlimited

Description of the activity
Everyone stands in a circle. One by one they introduce themselves by linking their first name to an adjective which says something about their character. For instance:
- Active Ally
- Jolly Joseph
- Creative Chris

In round two, people in the circle introduce each other: "Next to me is Jolly Joseph," until you have gone round the whole circle.

Tips & directions
Once everyone in the group has started to get to know each other a bit, you can ask people to come up with adjectives that fit their neighbors' personalities.

Variations
Turn it into a competitive game: how many names and alliterations can someone remember?

LEADING THE BLIND

● *Renatus Hoogenraad's favorite exercise*

Objective to trust your partner
Summary working in pairs, the participants lead their
blindfolded partner around the room
Duration 15–20 minutes
Number of participants unlimited (the exercise is done in pairs)

Description of the activity

Divide the group into pairs. Person A stands in front of person
B. B closes his eyes and places his left hand on A's right
shoulder. A starts to lead B around the room. A is responsible
for B's safety (make sure you emphasize this!) Once B's hand
feels heavier on A's shoulder, this is an indication of B's trust in
A. When this happens, you can make small changes to the way
people are moving around the room (slow - fast, stooped over -
upright, backwards – forwards.) After a while, ask the partners
to switch places.

Tips & directions

1. The number one rule which applies to this exercise is that
   you must not spoil the experience for the other person, or to
   put it in positive terms: look after each other. Make sure you
   keep an eye on groups with a competitive streak as they may
   have a tendency to make things extra difficult for the blind
   person.
2. After the exercise, ask if anyone cheated, did they feel brave
   enough to keep their eyes completely shut, when did they
   feel they could, when didn't they?
3. Which is easier, leading or following?

LET'S GO!

Objective to close the session together with great positive energy

Summary the participants all shout out "Let's go!" very loudly

Duration 3 minutes

Number of participants unlimited

Description of the activity

The participants stand in a circle, arms around each other's shoulders. At the trainer's signal, everyone shouts out "Let's go!" three times in a very loud voice. After the third time, all participants jump up in the air together and cheer as loudly as possible.

LETTER H

➲ *Bobbi Block's favorite exercise*

Objective to come up with more ideas, diverging,
having body contact
Summary form the letter H in as many ways as possible
Duration 10 minutes
Number of participants unlimited

Description of the activity
Get into pairs (if odd, one group of three). Spread out.
Tell group they have 7 seconds to make the letter H with their
bodies. Tell them to freeze in their 'H' and also look around
at each other. Then relax. Tell them they now have 7 seconds
to form.... the Letter H... a different way! Tell them they now
have 7 seconds to form.... the letter 'H'... a different way!
Do this again and again ... at least five or six times.
Countdown the 7 seconds immediately after saying 'go!', and
after each round, say 'look around.' If they are stuck for any
reason, gently coach them to jump into action, using all parts
of their bodies. You should have capitol Hs first, then some will
start making lower case hs, then some will lay on the floor and
hopefully some will do some outrageous things (handstands!)
to get new approaches to the task.

Tips & directions
- Tell the participants that they can make a partial offer + trust
  your partner to build on it
- Be inspired by the people around you and learn from them
- Debriefing: Simply ask: why did we do this activity? They
  will probably tell you: creative thinking; teamwork and
  collaboration; there's more than one way to achieve the
  same goal; sometimes the 3rd or 4th 'answer' is the one you

like the best; jumping in without thinking, be inspired by the people around you and learn from them, and more. This activity has many layers; depending on the objectives of the overall program in which you do this exercise, focus on the debrief areas which apply.

- Highlight that they accomplished this task by making 'partial offers': under the time constraint, they didn't have time to conceptualize the entire 'H' so they simply made a partial physical offer and trusted their partner to build on it with another partial offer, back and forth, until the task was complete: this is true collaborative creation.

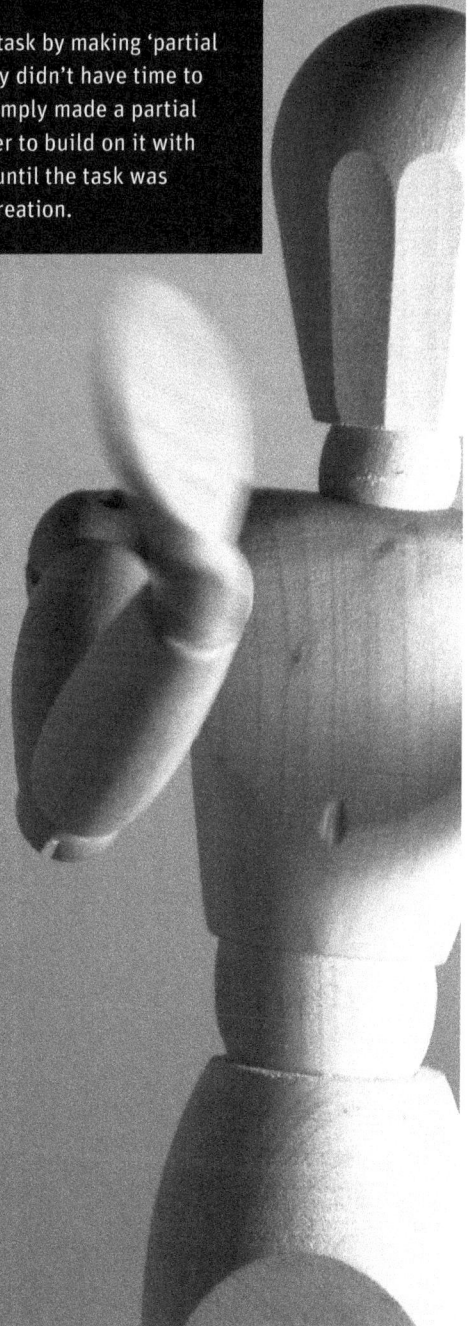

LINE-UP

Objective to get to know each other by asking various questions
Summary to arrange a group of people in a line as quickly
as possible
Duration 10–15 minutes
Number of participants unlimited

Description of the activity
The whole group stands in the performance area. Instruct them
to line themselves up as quickly as possible in a particular
order, for instance alphabetically by first name, alphabetically
by surname, etcetera. The possibilities are endless.
1. shoe size
2. age
3. number of years with the company
4. gross salary
5. number of kilometers driven annually
6. number of sandwiches eaten for lunch

Tips & directions
1. To make it exciting, set a time limit for the task: for instance,
   one minute.
2. Participants who not are lined up correctly must drop out,
   or sing a song, or do a different forfeit.
3. If the group does not quite know each other yet, give the
   participants another minute or so to talk to their neighbors
   to their immediate left and right after the line-up has been
   formed
4. You could also ask the participants to line up based on a
   theme linked to the contents of the course or workshop.
   For instance, in a creative session, you could ask them to
   line up in order of creativity.

MACHINE

Objective to accept ideas, to let go of your own plan, teamwork, flexible association
Summary the participants all work together to build a big imaginary machine
Duration at least 10 minutes
Number of participants 5–25

Description of the activity

Everyone stands in a circle. One (random) person moves to the middle of the circle and starts making a movement and noise which he keeps repeating. A second person joins him and makes a movement and noise which links into the first one. Do this until everyone is in the middle of the circle and you have created one big machine.

Tips & directions

Ask the participants to make up a machine beforehand that does not exist yet (for instance, a cigarette-butt-collecting machine, an automatic bottle opener) and then go on to create this machine.

It is fun to make the machine speed up at some point (once everyone has a 'function') and to let the machine fall apart. Or you could operate the machine at a slower and slower speed until everyone is standing still.

MINI-MAX

Objective to explore new points of view by maxing situations up or playing them down in the extreme
Summary act out a particular situation and max it up or play it down in the extreme
Duration at least 10 minutes
Number of participants 2 to 5 actors – the rest are the audience

Description of the activity

Ask two to five actors to act out a typical situation related to a problem. Give them a few minutes to do this and then ask them to act it out, maxing things up or playing them down in the extreme. So a certain aspect is completely blown up out of proportion or, on the contrary, totally minimized.

MIRROR MIRROR

↪ *Burgert Kirsten's favorite exercise*

Objective let participants experience giving and taking control and the power of co-creative flow.
Summary in pairs participants mirror each other's movement. In the first two rounds only one player is in control. In the third round they share the control.
Duration 15 minutes
Number of participants Pairs

Description of the activity

Ask everyone to pair up with another person and stand facing each other. Each pair should decide who will be A and who will be B. Tell them that A is a person looking into a mirror and B is the mirror. B should therefore copy A's exact movement. After a few minutes tell them to switch. A is now the mirror and B the person looking into the mirror.

After B has had a chance to lead for a few minutes, tell them that they have to now both lead and follow at the same time. They are therefore both looking into the mirror and being the mirror simultaneously. Now it gets really interesting. For it to work both need to take the lead and give up the lead, giving and taking control the whole time. If the participants trust each other and are completely present in the moment they will go into a state of flow in which control will dissolve.

Tips & directions

- The idea is not that the participants should try and outwit each other by making sudden movements. The idea is that they work together and move like they are one so that an observer wouldn't be able to see who is leading and who is following.

- It works best if the participants make smooth movements, not quick jerky movements.
- Tell the participants to do the exercise in complete silence.

Note about control and leadership
Taking control is about taking initiative, while giving up control is about letting go of your own idea when it is no longer serving the bigger picture. Some people are natural control freaks (or more commonly referred to as a natural leader) others are natural fence sitters (commonly referred to as natural followers). Both control freaks and fence sitters are often driven by fear and a lack of trust. The art of leadership is about knowing when to take control and knowing when to let go. If you are a control freak you need to learn to let go and trust others. If you are a fence sitter you need to take initiative and trust your own abilities.

Variations
Stand in a circle. Every person focuses his attention on another person. Every person looks at a particular person and is looked at by someone else. You then start to copy all movements and facial expressions of the person you are focusing on. The aim of this exercise is that no one feels like initiating a movement; you just mirror the person you are focused on (so when this person moves, you copy his movement). This is a perfect exercise to show how much we actually 'move' (consciously and subconsciously) when the task is in fact not to initiate any movement at all.

ONE CLAP

Objective closing the event with one clap
Summary the whole audience claps once at the same time
Duration 2 minutes
Number of participants unlimited

Description of the exercise

This is a great exercise to do at the end of an event when the audience has already applauded a few times for all the organizers, speakers, and others. Ask the audience to stand up and open their arms. Explain that the whole audience is going to clap once but the challenge is to do it at the same time without agreeing on when the clap is going to happen. You will also participate and try to build up the tension (but don't take the lead). Most of the time, somewhere between 5 and 10 seconds, everybody will clap at the same time. If the clap doesn't happen at the same time, invite the audience to try it again and ask them to concentrate and connect with the 'energy.' Most of the time, the second time, it will go even better.

ONE WORD AT A TIME

Objective acceptance, teamwork
Summary as a group, tell a story one word at a time
Duration 10 minutes
Number of participants group of 10 people

Description of the activity

Stand in a circle and ask people to give you the title of a story that does not exist. The group then starts to create a story, one word at a time, where every participant is allowed to say one word and the next word is added by his neighbor. It is important to point out that the structure of the sentence and logical content have to be right.

Tips & directions

- Create a logical, simple story instead of adding crazy elements.
- Each person can only add one word at a time. Some people like to stay in control and call out two or three words.
- When a sentence has a logical ending, you can call out 'full stop.'

ORACLE

Objective to think up new angles or ideas based on
the oracle's answers
Summary 2 people form 1 identity — the oracle —
and respond as one person to questions from the others
Duration 15 minutes — 3 to 5 minutes per group
(2 people form a small group to become the oracle)
Number of participants 2

Description of the activity
Select two participants and ask them to stand in front of the
group. Instruct them to speak as one person — they always
have to speak simultaneously but without deciding beforehand
who leads and who follows.
Next, ask a few simple questions about the subject. The other
people present can subsequently also ask the oracle some
questions.

Do this for about three to five minutes. After this, ask everyone
present to write down any ideas based on the oracle's answers.
If you have enough time, you can also form a different group to
play the oracle and then the whole process starts again.

Tips & directions
- Tell the participants that this is a very difficult exercise and
  that it is totally okay if they make mistakes.
- The trick to speaking as one is to mirror each other's mouths.
  You may have to coach the participants a little in the begin-
  ning to pay more attention to each other.
- Encourage the people who form the group to talk as quickly
  as possible but always simultaneously.
- Encourage the people who form the oracle to alternate the
  leader and follower roles.

- When a sentence makes absolutely no sense whatsoever or the participants are not speaking simultaneously, ask them to repeat their answer.
- Ask lots of questions and suggest that the people who form the oracle keep the answers short.

ORCHESTRA

Objective warming up
Summary create a rhythm ('song') with the whole audience
Duration 10 minutes
Number of participants unlimited

Description of the exercise

Divide the audience into three or four groups and give every group a sound (or a kind of body drum). Every sound is related to a kind of movement that you make on the stage (e.g. raising your left hand means that group 1 has to make their sound, raising your right hand is group 2, moving your left leg is group 3) and then try to make a composition together with the audience.

Variations

Give the men and the women a different sound and play with that. Tell them they are members of a wild tribe, the women go 'Ugh' when you raise your left hand and the men go 'Aargh'.

PASS THE CLAP

Objective to accept ideas, teamwork
Summary simple starting exercise where participants stand
in a circle and pass on a handclap to their neighbor
Duration minimum 10 minutes
Number of participants 10–25 in a circle

Description of the activity

Everyone stands in a circle. Someone starts off the exercise
by clapping his hands once while looking at his neighbor.
The neighbor in question turns to the person standing to his
other side, makes eye contact and passes the clap on. This way,
the clap is passed around the circle. Once the participants have
got the hang of this, someone could decide not to turn to his
other neighbor but rather to pass the clap back to the giver.
This way, the clap goes around the circle in the other direction.

Tips & directions

- Make sure that the participants stick to the task and do not
  try to make up all sorts of different versions straightaway.
- Try to get into a single rhythm.
- Try to mix things up by changing the speed and tempo.
- Do not introduce the idea of passing the clap back to the
  giver until later in the exercise.
- When two participants keep passing the clap back and forth
  to each other, make sure you intervene. Explain that when
  they do this, they are the only two people who are playing
  and that the rest of the group is just watching. This is annoying
  for the people watching.
- If the group is too big for the room, take the game outside or
  divide the group into two circles.

Variations

- Pass on a jump instead of a clap. The participant jumps, making a quarter of a turn in the air to the right (or left) and looks at his neighbor. This person in turn jumps up in the air to pass the jump on to the next person.
- Once everyone has got the hang of the exercise, you could start up claps in several places at once in the circle.

PASS THE PATTERNS

Objective create a fairly complex production system and research what cooperation, clear communication, ownership and creativity can mean for such a system.

Summary start up a production setting where three different patterns are sustained throughout the exercise. Buildup is one pattern at a time.

Duration 10–20 minutes

Number of participants 8–20

Description of the exercise

Build three patterns in the following way:

Everyone in the group raises their hands. One person starts by passing the word for a fruit or vegetable to someone with their arm up. This person lowers his or her own arm. The person receiving this word passes a new vegetable or fruit to someone with their arm still up and lowers his/her arm. Repeat this until no one is left with their arm up. The last person passes to the one who started the pattern. Make sure all the fruits and vegetables are different. Repeat this pattern a couple of times so that the group knows it well.

Install a different pattern with countries and cities. Let people pass these to someone new. Repeat this pattern until the group knows it well.

Start up the first pattern while this second pattern is going and examine what emerges. The goal is to have the two patterns go around simultaneously.

If these two patterns start going round fairly well introduce a third pattern in a similar way. This time, participants do not pass a word, but instead walk towards someone with their arm up.

Repeat this pattern until it is well known, then give the group the responsibility to start up the other two patterns as well and to keep all three patterns going.

Tips and tricks

- Put the focus on strong communication and resilience. You can pretend that each word passed brings in $50000 for the organization. What can be done in order to lose as little profit as possible?
- Discuss the ownership of the transaction (a transaction is the passing and receiving of a word or the movement of a participant to a new location.) The ownership lies on both sides of the transaction.
- Demonstrate the importance of resilience. If participants start to look where something goes wrong every time they lose a pattern, the entire production process is halted every time. Better to help each other to pick up the pieces: when noticing a pattern has stopped just simply relaunch it, and when someone notices the same pattern is going twice, stop one when it comes to you, unless there is a clear pattern in the failure (someone never receives a word from a certain category.) Find ways to solve problems quickly and efficiently.
- Look at what is happening, not who is to blame.

PASS THE ZAP!

● *Vic McWaters' favorite exercise*

Objective to experience making quick choices in the moment, failing, and learning and improving from practice and making mistakes. Focus and attention

Summary a sound and movement game played in a circle which starts easy and gradually becomes more complicated as new elements are introduced

Duration 10–30 minutes

Number of participants 6–50

Description of the activity

Ask people to stand in a circle with some space between each person.

Round 1 Introduce the Zap!
A Zap! passes in either direction around the circle. It includes a hand clap, the sound Zap! and making eye contact with the person you are passing the Zap! to. Send the Zap! around the circle in one direction, and then explain that you can choose to change direction if you want when you have control of the Zap!

Round 2 Introduce the Whoosh!
Stop the game and introduce the next element known as a Whoosh! A Whoosh! can only be sent across the circle. Explain that when you have control of the game you can either send a Zap! either direction around the circle or transform it to a Whoosh! and send it across the circle.

Round 3 Introduce the Boing!
Stop the game and introduce the third and final element – the Boing! When someone sends a Whoosh! at you, you can reject it by raising both hands and saying Boing! The control of the

game returns to the sender who can then choose to send another Whoosh! to someone else or to transform it into a Zap!

Tips & directions

- As the game becomes more complicated there is a greater need to pay attention, stay in the moment and to try not to block your choices.
- Obviously the Boing! option is all about blocking. This can be a useful debrief conversation.
- It is also a good game for making mistakes — and celebrating them — as many mistakes will be made!
- It is also about commitment. Players need to choose an action and commit to it. Often in the first round of Zap! players will be low energy. Encourage more commitment.
- Can also be used to explore looking after others — to what extent did players just want to get rid of control of the game to someone else compared with making sure the receiver was aware and ready?
- Can speed up and slow down the game as needed.
- Allow some time to debrief, as no matter how the game is used and in which context, there are usually some useful insights about individual and group behavior.

PERFECT BOSS

⊕ *Matt Weinstein's favorite exercise*

Objective creating a positive atmosphere
Summary creating a positive atmosphere by giving compliments and learning to delegate
Duration 10 minutes
Number of participants unlimited (you need some open space)

Description of the exercise
Form groups of three people and decide who is A, B and C. Person A is the boss and the two other people are loyal employees. The boss is going to give compliments to the other people in the room but you delegate those tasks to your employees (e.g. "Go over to Mary and tell her I think she has a great smile, and come right back to me," or "I want you to find somebody who was not born in this city and thank him or her for coming to this meeting today," or "Find five different people who you don't know at all, shake their hands and introduce yourself to them.") Before you start giving the compliments, connect as a team and then do this exercise for 1 minute. After the minute, the two employees return to the boss and now the boss can ask the employees to do something supportive for him for 30 seconds (e.g. a dual backrub, words of praise.) Then person B becomes the boss and after that, person C.

Source Matt Weinstein

PRESENT

Objective suspension of judgment, acceptance
Summary you take it in turns to give each other a present and
the receiver names it, making it concrete
Duration 10 minutes
Number of participants unlimited (the exercise is done in pairs)

Description of the activity

Pair up with a partner. Every person gives his partner a present.
To give a present, you simply open your arms and hands to
indicate that you are holding something. Try not to think about
what you are holding, just give the present to your fellow actor.
The person who receives the present, gives it a name — the first
thing that comes to mind. Say something like 'Wow, thanks, it's
a ...' after which you immediately stop and give a present to the
other person. Try to also do this exercise as quickly as possible.
It really does not matter what you give or what the other person
receives.

Tips & directions

• The person receiving the present is always very positive
  about the present — after all, he always decides himself
  what he gets.
• Speed is once again important. Once the present has been
  'identified,' it is time for the next idea to be given.

PROBLEM WALK

Objective to increase the knowledge and involvement of the participants with regard to a problem
Summary the participants literally decide what their position is with respect to the problem owner
Duration 15–30 minutes.
Number of participants unlimited

Description of the activity
The problem owner stands in the middle of a big circle formed by the participants. The problem owner describes the problem. The participants then go on to ask questions. When the problem starts getting clearer to the participants as the briefing unfolds, they move closer to the problem owner and the distance between the participants and problem owner decreases.
The participants only move forwards if they have received a satisfactory answer to their question and if they are willing to contribute towards resolving the problem.

Tips & directions
- As a participant, you literally have to take a position and decide on your distance to the problem owner.
- The problem owner can also stand opposite the rest of the group. The participants of the group take it in turns to ask the problem owner questions for clarification. If the answer is satisfactory, the participant takes a step towards the problem owner. The other members of the group may also take a step forwards but you can only step forwards if you feel that you grasp the problem and also wish to contribute to the solution of the problem.
- As the trainer, write down the most important findings from the group.

PSSSSSSHHHT

Objective to warm up in a physical, playful manner, to practice concentration
Summary in pairs, you make physical movements and you make a 'shooting motion' when you have made the same movement as your partner
Duration 5 to 10 minutes
Number of participants unlimited (the exercise is done in pairs)

Description of the activity
Pair up with a partner and stand opposite each other. Both of you move your arms to the left, right, or upwards at a set rhythm (slowly at first). In between movements, slap your thighs. All this is done independently of each other. When you both happen to make a movement in the same direction, make a shooting motion at each other (remember to slap your thighs first) and shout 'psssssshhht'. Slap your thighs once more and carry on with the exercise.

Tips & directions
Once the participants have got into a groove, challenge them to up the tempo.

RAIN

Objective to collectively close a session with lots of positive energy
Summary the participants gradually build up an applause, reproducing the sound of a rain shower
Duration 10 minutes
Number of participants unlimited

Description of the activity
Everyone stands in a circle. The trainer explains that the group is going to gradually build up a full applause, reproducing the sound of a refreshing rain shower.

The participants start off by rubbing their hands together. Next, they click their fingers before moving on to clapping the fingers of both hands together. Then, they tap the palms of their hands with two fingers, after which they clap their hands together. Next, everyone stamps their feet.

The rain shower reaches its climax, a towering crescendo of sound. The process is then reversed as the group simulates the gradual dying down of the rain shower.

REVERSE MUSICAL CHAIRS

Objective to encourage initial physical contact in a playful way
Summary a fun take on an old favorite, reverse musical chairs
Duration 10–30 minutes, depending on the size of the group
Number of participants 10–25 (depending on the number
of chairs)

Description of the activity
This exercise is very much like musical chairs except for the
fact that while the number of chairs decreases, everyone still
stays in the game. There are no losers. Put out the same number
of chairs, minus one, in the room as there are people. Then
put on some music. When the music stops, everyone has to sit
down on a chair. A participant who is left standing has to try,
in one way or another, to break contact with the floor as quickly
as possible (for instance, by sitting on someone's lap.) Next,
remove another chair, start the music and carry on with the
game. Do this until only one chair remains and everyone has
to sit on this one chair.

Tips & directions
• Be careful to avoid accidents. Sometimes, participants get
  so enthusiastic that they become careless.
• Contact with the floor may also be broken in other ways.
  Tables, bags, curtains, instructors, anything goes, providing
  no one gets hurt or nothing gets irreparably damaged.

ROCK-PAPER-SCISSORS

Objective Raising the energy in a large group, being a leader and supporting a leader
Summary The group plays Rock-Paper-Scissors in pairs. The winners form new pairs, while the others cheer them on.
Duration 5 minutes
Number of participants large groups

Description of the activity

Divide the group in pairs. Each pair will play Rock-Paper-Scissors as follows. The pairs count to three (1-2-3-go) and on "go," they will stretch out their hand symbolizing a rock (fist), scissors (two fingers) or paper (outstretched fingers). Rock beats scissors, scissors beats paper and paper beats rock. On a draw, the players play again. After a game, the loser will join the winner and support them by chanting his or her name and shouting encouragements. Together, they will find another group of people and the two winners will play again. The winner of this game will now have three followers. This will continue until the last two people, each with many followers, play the game.

Tips & directions

This is a fast exercise that will raise the energy in a large group very quickly. It can also be used to discuss leadership.

Source Matt Weinstein

SEVEN STRANGE QUESTIONS

Objective to get to know each other based on a list of strange questions
Summary give each other answers to strange questions
Duration 5 to 15 minutes
Number of participants unlimited

Description of the exercise
Prepare in advance seven strange questions related to the topic of the event. Before showing the questions (on a slide) to the participants, ask the participants to think of a number between 1 and 7. Let them form pairs and decide who is A and B. Then you show the 7 questions and A has to ask B the question that corresponds with their number. After one minute they have to switch so B asks A his question. Here are some examples of questions that can be adapted, depending on the topic.

1. What will you be doing in 2015?
2. What was your most beautiful moment in the last month?
3. If you had to move to another planet, what would you take with you?
4. If somebody wrote a book about you, what would be the title?
5. To which time period would you go if you had a time machine?
6. What did you want to be when you were a child?
7. What is a special gift that you have?

SHOOT-OUT

Objective to learn names, physical warm-up
Summary quick reaction game involving acceptance
Duration 10 minutes
Number of participants about 10 participants per circle

Description of the activity
Everyone stands in a circle and shapes each hand into a gun.
The facilitator stands in the middle and calls out someone's
name. This person has to duck as quickly as possible. His
neighbors to the left and right of him have to shoot each other
as quickly as possible. The person who shoots last dies (making
horrible dying noises.) If it is not clear who was the faster out
of the two gunslingers, both die. Remember to explain clearly
that it is also about 'the act of dying.' This ritual is part of the
exercise, so enjoy your 'death.' The dead person walks (or
crawls) out of the circle and is allowed to call out a name. When
there are only two people left, they have to stand back to back.
When they are given a signal, they have to walk away from each
other until the signal is given that they can turn around and
shoot.

Tips & directions
The exercise is not about winning the game. Make sure that the
emphasis is not on winning. Graciousness and acceptance play
a major part in this exercise. When two people shoot at about
the same time, is someone gracious, letting the other person
live? Or do both people die? If there is an argument about who
shot first, the facilitator should intervene and send the most
competitive person out of the circle.

SHOUT NUMBERS

● *(One of) Shawn Kinley's favorite exercises*

Objective a tool to work on Judgement Behaviour
and decision making
Summary quick reaction game involving acceptance,
self-sacrifice and choice
Duration 10 minutes
Number of participants unlimited

Description of the activity
You have a room full of people. Ask them to get together in sub-groups - according the number that you will tell them. All they need to do is get together in that group (e.g. "four!" – Groups of four.) Tell them that they have a limited time to get into that group.

Those who are in groups too big or groups too small will be eliminated after a pre-determined time. You can count down 3-2-1 and make a horrible failure sound to let them know time is up.

Start slow. Give them some element of success. Then speed up and start to eliminate groups. What do you see? Individuals become super-efficient at finding their group. They race together, towards people they would originally not have chosen. They laugh as they do it. Now we have an environment where people are joyfully moving forward. There is no subtle exclusion or favoritism going on anymore.

It's an unfair game of course because eventually you might be yelling out "four!" or "two" for example in a room of nine people. If that extra person jumps into a complete group, that entire group is thrown out. People learn to take care of the group even if it doesn't benefit them. In this situation, the person socially succeeds by allowing self-sacrifice.

They learn quick and efficient awareness to see. If two people stay out in the above scenario with the idea of self sacrifice then one of those groups of four will be short a person. The decision is made quickly to correct the problem because they know that the timer is ticking.

For children who choose only their friend or don't want to be paired up with a boy or a girl, this exercise eliminates the psychological barrier. For business people it begins to correct status problems common in unbalanced peer structure groups.

Source *Shawn Kinley*

SNAP

⊃ *Paul Z Jackson's favorite exercise*

Objective stimulating creativity skills
Summary stimulate creative thinking by playing a game with
imaginary cards
Duration 10 minutes
Number of participants unlimited

Description of the exercise
Invite the participants to form pairs. The facilitator says,
"You remember the children's card game where you have to
match up pairs with your partner. The game is called 'snap,'
because when you both turn over the same card as each other,
the first person to say 'Snap' wins the pile of cards.

"We don't have real cards here, so we shall use imaginary
cards. This pack here is an Animal cards pack. Let's share them
out, half each, and we each turn one over at a time, and tell our
partner the name of the card. It is important to do the naming
simultaneously — and remember, if it's the same card, you say
'Snap' to win."

Both players turn imaginary cards and name the card they are
turning: 'Dog, cat, elephant...' until they say the same name,
when one calls 'Snap' — and then the process repeats.

After a few minutes, signal to change partners, and also to
change the deck of cards. You might use 'countries,' 'colors,'
'football teams' or any other category variations.
We recommend demonstrating the activity with a volunteer.

Source Paul Z Jackson

SOLUTION WALK

Objective to clarify and refine a top concept
Summary indicate through physical distance whether you
feel a particular concept is clear or not so the concept can
be refined if need be
Duration at least 10 minutes
Number of participants unlimited

Description of the activity
Select a particular solution and a problem owner. The other
members of the group form a circle around the problem owner
and by asking questions can contribute towards making the
solution more concrete. The participants move closer to the
problem owner as the solution becomes clearer to them. The
closer the participants are to the problem owner, the clearer
and more concrete the solution is.

Tips & directions
The 'commitment walk' follows on very closely from this exercise.

SPEAK AS ONE

Objective acceptance, teamwork
Summary several people speak as if they were one person
Duration 10 to 15 minutes
Number of participants unlimited (the exercise is done in small groups of 2 to 4 people)

Description of the activity

In groups of two to four people, the participants tell a story, ask questions or explain a certain process while copying each other verbally. To make things easier, it helps for people of the same group to stand closely together (possibly linking arms). So the idea is that everyone in the group talks at the same time, despite not knowing what the other people in their group are going to say. In the beginning, it is therefore very important to speak slowly so that the whole group can follow. Point out that you can both lead and follow in this exercise. Nothing is agreed in advance as to who will lead and who will follow. You can place two groups opposite each other and let them tell a story.

STATUE EXHIBITION

Objective to develop new ideas through statues
Summary two participants take up changing positions while those watching make associations based on what they are seeing
Duration minimum 20 minutes
Number of participants two participants as statues, the rest of the group watches and writes down or calls out any ideas they come up with as a result of looking at the statues

Description of the activity
Two people stand in front of the group and move about. When the facilitator calls 'stop,' they have to stand as still as a statue. The spectators look at the statues and call out any associations they make as a result of what they are seeing.

Tips & directions
- When ideas run dry, the statues take up a new position.
- Swap actors and spectators around.
- Create a group of statues with several actors.
- A spectator can take the place of a figure in the statues group by tagging him out and taking up his position.
- The statues can start to move about (as a reaction to the associations from the spectators) and a short scene can be created.

Variations
Ask a 'guide' to explain what the statues depict.

STATUS RECEPTION

Objective nonverbal communication, to look at things
from other angles
Summary creating characters based on a change in status
Duration 10 minutes
Number of participants unlimited

Description of the activity
Divide the group into two subgroups. The people in group A
have a high status and are asked to act accordingly (hold head
up high, look people in the eyes, straight shoulders, walk
around in a dignified way,) and those in group B have a low
status (retiring, frequently touching their head and body,
avoiding eye contact with everyone.) Make sure people really
immerse themselves in their roles and tell them that they
are at a reception — they are allowed to engage in short
conversations.

Tips & directions
- Compile a list of characteristics related to high and low
  status beforehand.
- Afterwards, collect different people's thoughts and findings.
  What status suits them best in real life (everyone has a
  'natural' status)? You can make changes to the status level
  by introducing a scale from 1 to 10. At level 1, your status
  is still fairly neutral and the higher you rise up the scale,
  the stronger your status manifests itself.

Variations
- Instead of a reception, you could let the participants act out
  a short scene between two people sitting on a bench and
  change the status every now and again.
- Ask the participants to greet each other in a 'high' and 'low'
  way.

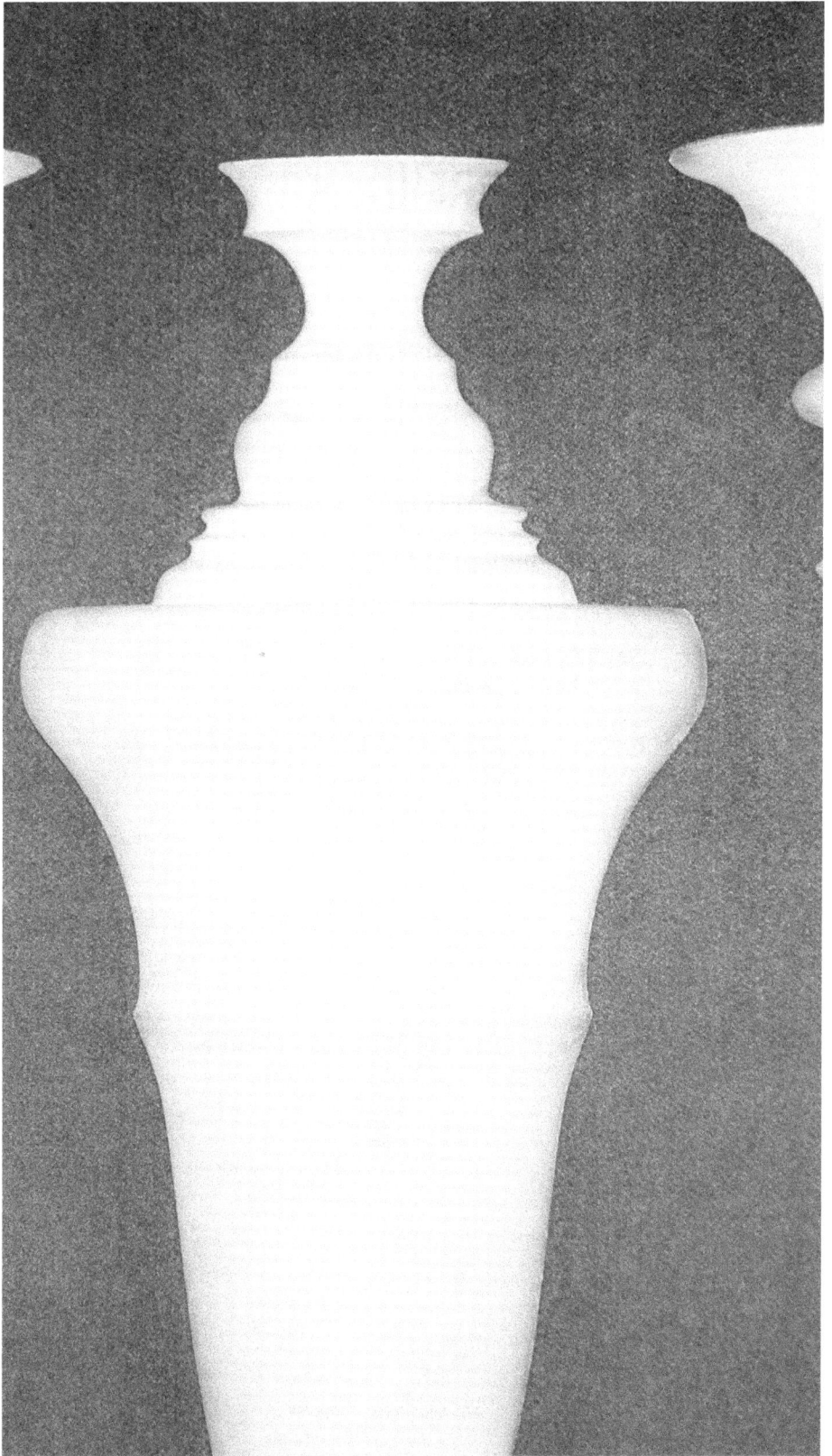

SUPER PRESIDENT

● *Hikaru Hie's favorite exercise*

Objective learn positive thinking, focus on solutions, learn and master 'Yes, and,' cooperate on solutions, accept ideas and situations.

Summary this game can be used to raise self-confidence as well as to introduce way of positive thinking by using 'Yes, and' in any difficult situations or problems.

Duration 15–20 minutes

Number of participants unlimited (the exercise is done in small groups)

Description of the activity

Before the game, write a scenario on a whiteboard like the following;

Employee:	Super President! We have a problem.
SP:	What is it? (look confident and smile)
E:	(make up a problem)
SP:	That sounds super! (make up a solution)

All employees:	How super you are!
	(repeat the idea from Super President, then add more ideas to it)
SP:	How super YOU are too!! Then let's do that!

Divide the participants into small groups of three to five people. People within each small group have to appoint the Super President.

The facilitator decides what kind of company or organization it is. Then ask the participants to follow the scenario and add the ideas.

Here's an example of how the conversation might go if the facilitator decides the situation is at achocolate company.

Employee:	Super President! We have a problem.
SP:	What is it?
E:	The Japanese government decided not to import any cacao anymore.
SP:	That sounds great! Let's try to roast soybeans and create a new healthy chocolate. (It does not have to be the best solution, but the point is to say something and take it positively.)
All Employees:	How super you are! We are going to invent healthy soy chocolate. Then we can export it to other countries where many health conscious people live.
TSP:	How super YOU are too!! Then let's do that!

Tips and Directions

Avoid situations which are too close to the one of the participants. For example, if the participants are the employees of an IT company, don't introduce situations having to do with IT.

TALK IN METAPHORS

Objective understand and experience the difference between direct and indirect communication
Summary participants play a short scene twice, first with direct and factual lines, then in indirect or metaphorical language
Duration 20–30 minutes
Number of participants two players, a facilitator and audience.

Description of the activity
The trainer asks two participants to play a simple scene with a few lines (e.g. buying a roll in a bakery).
The dialogue should be as factual as possible:

—Good morning, sir!
—Good morning, baker!
—Can I have a roll please?
—Yes.
—How much does it cost?
—2.50.

In the second round the players are allowed only to talk in indirect sentences. Players must describe instead of mentioning the items directly. They have to talk in the third person, they can never ask directly what they want, but have to let the other discover their wishes.

In the debrief, after both scenes, the trainer can ask the participants, what differences they saw in the scenes, and what were the advantages and disadvantages of both scenes. Make sure that the participants do not judge the different types of communication.

Tips & directions

Another version of this exercise is to play the second round using a metaphor. The players have to continue in the metaphor as long as possible. Possible metaphors:

- penguins on the North Pole
- a deck of playing cards
- a game of chess
- driving a vehicle

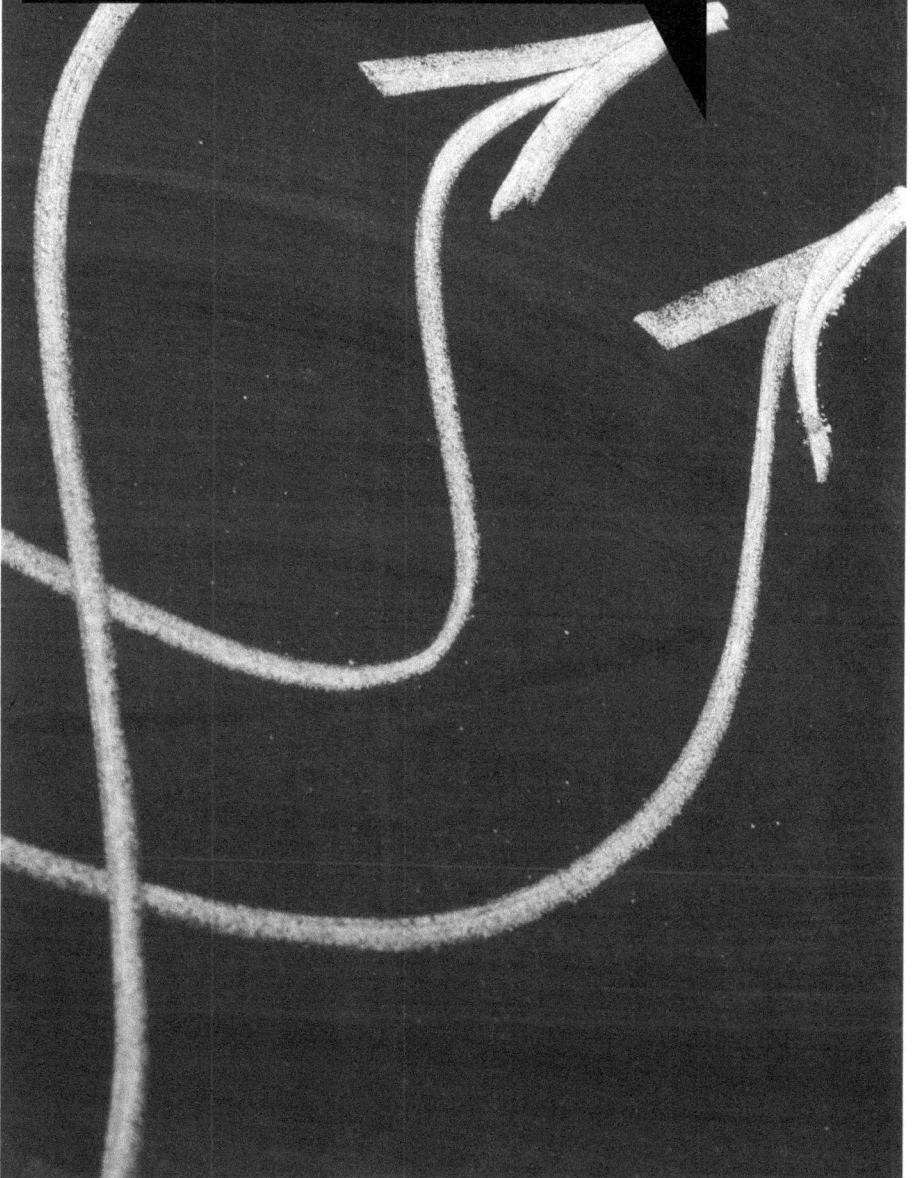

THOUGHT EXPERIMENT

Objective imagining how you behave in another environment
Summary the group acts out how they would behave after
certain changes
Duration 20 minutes
Number of participants unlimited (allow for enough room)

Description of the activity

Instruct the participants to walk randomly through the room
(avoid patterns such as all participant walking in the same
circle). Ask the participants to greet each other shortly as they
meet. Now introduce a new situation, such as: "walk around
as if your team just won the championship" or "Walk around
as if you are in a scary forest". Depending on the goal of the
training, you can let the changes become ever more realistic.
This is a very good exercise to use if your participants are
faced with organizational change. Let them walk around and
greet each other as they would in the new organization. E.g.
if the organizational change is that people have become more
entrepreneurial,
let the participant walk around as entrepreneurs.

TRIANGLES

● *André Besseling's favorite exercise*

Objective networking exercise, warming up
Summary form an equilateral triangle in groups of three people
Duration 3 minutes plus time for debrief
Number of participants unlimited (at least 7)

Description of the activity
Ask the participants to stand in an open space and they have to pick two other people. Don't point or say who those people are, but try to make an equilateral triangle with those people. Give a time limit of three minutes. It is mathematically possible to reach a figure where everybody is standing still. Whether people found the figure or not, stop after a maximum of three minutes.

You will notice that everybody will be moving in the beginning but after a while the whole group starts to move slower (unless one person moves fast) and can even come to standstill.

Tips and directions
In the debriefing, you can focus on the constant movement in the exercise. How did this make people feel? Some people will even try to influence other people to move according to their wishes. This behavior often mirrors the behavior in normal work processes. When debriefing on leadership, emphasize the circle of influence people have. This exercise works best when focusing on your own influence by keeping in motion, instead of trying to influence others.
The exercise works best when you allow people to talk. This way, social processes can be observed better.

WALKING BY NUMBERS

Objective nonverbal communication, to pay attention to each other, to follow and lead
Summary walk around the room based on a set number of participants allowed to walk at once
Duration 10 minutes
Number of participants groups of 10 people

Description of the activity

All participants spread out randomly in the room. The arrangement is that only one person at a time may be walking. When someone is walking, all the others have to stand still. The person who is walking may decide to stop suddenly and then someone else (only one person) has to start walking.
As the facilitator, you can decide at a certain point in the game to increase the number of people allowed to walk at once.

Tips & directions

- In order to maintain concentration, it helps if people are quiet.
- Tell the participants to make clear decisions. When you start walking, make sure you are clearly walking. If you want to stop walking, make sure to stop immediately.
- It is important that no agreements are made regarding the following and leading aspect of the exercise.

WHAT ARE YOU DOING?

Objective acceptance, suspension of judgment, to understand that it is okay to make mistakes
Summary game where the action and the naming of the action do not match up
Duration 15 minutes
Number of participants unlimited (the exercise is done in pairs)

Description of the activity

Pair up with a partner. Person A pretends to be doing a certain activity, for instance, cooking. Person B asks: 'What are you doing?' to which A responds by naming an activity which has nothing to do with cooking (for instance: 'I'm fishing'). Next, B pretends to fish. A then asks 'What are you doing?' to which B responds by naming a totally different activity and A again goes on to pretend to do this activity.

Tips & directions

- The activities people are acting out and naming should not belong to the same field (e.g. not all sports or kitchen related activities)
- Speed is very important in this exercise.

WHAT I LIKE ABOUT YOUR IDEA...

➔ *Sue Walden's favorite exercise*

Objective to invite people to practice finding value in each other's ideas. Excellent for leaders who want to encourage more participation from their teams

Summary one person proposes an initial idea, the second person reacts with "What I like about your idea is..." and finds something they authentically appreciate about the offered idea. After appreciating the idea, the second person adds to the plan by saying, "And..." This exercise introduces "Yes, and" and helps people to build the skill of finding what could work, the alternate skill to problem-spotting

Duration about 4-5 minutes so that the pairs have time to develop their plan and practice appreciating and adding.

Number of participants Any, best if even numbers

Description of the activity

Assign the pairs something to plan together: an outing, a vacation, a team meeting, etc. The exercise starts with one partner (A) saying 'Let's...' (do something short and simple that they could do together — e.g. go to the park, go to the movies...) Partner B says 'Yes, what I like about your idea is ... (something short and simple that they genuinely like about the idea, e.g. I love to be in nature.) "AND we could...'
(B adds something short and simple that moves the adventure forward: e.g. bring a Frisbee). A now follows the same script ("What I like about your idea is..."; then moving the adventure forward, "And we could...") They continue finding value and building the adventure together.

Tips & debrief

It helps to demonstrate it beforehand, and invite non-work situations to practice the skills. What might happen if you did this more often in your leadership role?

Source Sue Walden

198

WHAT SHAPE ARE YOU IN?

➔ *Yael Schy's favorite exercise*

Objective to allow participants to find shared moods with other members of their team, and to discuss the impact on the group.
Summary this movement-based exercise is a form of visual "check-in," which is good to use at the beginning of a group session. It allows participants to learn more about each other, by discovering shared moods and common themes among members of the group.
Duration Approximately 15 to 20 minutes.
Number of participants 10 to 50

Description of the activity

This learning experience is a form of visual 'check-in,' which is good to use at the beginning of any group session. It is a way of allowing participants to nonverbally get in touch with their current mood. By bringing their attention to their bodies, it enables participants to be more present and in the moment.

This exercise also allows participants to learn more about each other, by discovering shared moods and common themes among members of the group. The exercise can be used either with participants who do not know each other, as an 'ice-breaker' or to help an ongoing team to deepen their relationship.

1. Ask participants to find their own space in the room and to stand, making sure that each person has some space around himself or herself.
2. Ask each participant to reflect on what his/her current mood is. After a few moments, ask participants to each take on a body shape or gesture that reflects that mood.

3. Next, ask the participants to add a movement to the shape — one that still reflects their current mood — and to begin to move their body shape within their own space.
4. Now, ask the participants to continue the shape and motion and to move around the room, noticing the other people and what shapes and movements they are expressing.
5. Ask participants to each find several other people who have assumed a similar shape and/or movement and to form a small group with those people. (If there are several people left over who can't find anyone with a similar shape, ask those "unique shapes" to form a separate group. If there are only one or two people who are left over, ask them each to join a group that is the most similar to their shape/ movement.)
6. Ask the small groups to discuss within each group what each person's mood was and why they chose the shapes and movements that they did.
7. Have each group, in turn, demonstrate their shapes and movements to the larger group, and ask a spokesperson from each group to summarize the group discussion.

Tips & directions
Ask the following questions of participants to debrief the activity:
- How did you feel during the exercise?
- Did it make a difference in your mood to find other people with similar moods and shapes?
- How do you feel now?
- Did your mood change during the course of the exercise? If so, why?
- What did you learn about how your body reflects your mood?
- How might your moods and emotions impact your work?
- How can getting in touch with what you are feeling help you to better manage your moods and emotions in the workplace?

Variations

This exercise could be used for a variety of training objectives, including the following:

1. Emotional Intelligence: To help participants get in touch with their moods and emotions
2. Presentation Skills: To help participants become more aware of their body language
3. Cultural Diversity: To help participants explore cultural differences in the meaning of body language
4. Communication Skills: To help participants understand the impact of their moods and body language in communication
5. Teambuilding: To explore differences in body language among various personality types (use in conjunction with a personality type assessment tool)

Source *Yael Schy*

WHOOSH

Objective to accept ideas, teamwork
Summary a more chaotic and playful version of the pass-the-clap exercise
Duration minimum 10 minutes
Number of participants 10–25 in a circle

Description of the activity

Everyone stands in a circle. Someone starts off the exercise by making a wave motion towards his right-hand neighbor and making a 'whoosh' noise. This person then has to pass on the whoosh. You can also choose one of the following four sounds or motions:

1. Wow: both arms up in the air. The receiver throws both arms up in the air and shouts "Wow." The giver then has to pass on the whoosh in the opposite direction.
2. Zap: the giver points his arm at someone in the circle. This person then decides in which direction to pass on the whoosh.
3. Grooooovelicious: the person whose turn it is puts his hands up in the air. Everyone in the group follows suit, shouts "Grooooovelicious," crouches and stands back up again in a 'groovy' way. The person who started the Grooooovelicious continues with the whoosh.
4. Freak-out: everyone in the group puts their hands up in the air and moves, screaming and getting in each other's way, to a different spot in the circle. Once a new circle has been formed, the person who started the freak-out continues with the whoosh.

Tips & directions

- Make sure that the participants stick to the task and do not try to make up all sorts of different versions straightaway.
- Try to get into a single rhythm.
- Try to mix things up by changing the speed and tempo.
- Start by passing the whoosh on properly before introducing alternatives.
- When two participants keep passing a motion back and forth to each other, make sure you intervene. Explain that when they do this, they are the only two people who are playing while the rest of the group is just watching. This is annoying for the people watching because they are not able to participate at that time.

Variations

This is a very playful but powerful exercise and quickly shows who in the group is willing to participate, who is obstructive, etcetera. Based on this exercise (and also the handclap exercise), you can identify a number of elements which can also be found in a real organization (blocking, escapist behavior, accepting, being part of the team).

WORD ASSOCIATION CHAIN

Objective association, suspension of judgment
Summary create a chain of words through ongoing word association
Duration 10 minutes
Number of participants groups of 15 people

Description of the activity

Everyone stands in a big circle. Someone starts off the game by giving his right-hand neighbor a word. This person then associates another word with the given word and passes the association on to his neighbor. This creates a chain which travels around the circle.

Tips & directions

- Speed is important in this game — try to keep the speed up as much as possible so that people don't think too long, but realize that they will always come up with some idea or other without thinking.
- At the start of the exercise, you could agree that participants who fail to come up with an association straightaway call out a 'set' word. Use an easy word for this such as bicycle or apple. This gives people a sense of safety.

Variations

Instead of passing on a word, pass on an object. The idea is that the participants then go on to create associations related to the uses of the object. For instance, you pass on a pen: participant A pretends to write, participant B uses it as a stirrer, participant C pretends that the pen is a rocket, etcetera.

204

YES BUT, YES AND...

Objective teamwork, to accept ideas and build on other people's ideas
Summary experience the power of resistance ('Yes, but') and acceptance ('Yes, and')
Duration minimum 15 minutes
Number of participants unlimited (the exercise is done in pairs)

Description of the activity
Divide the group into pairs. Person A makes a suggestion to do something together with person B. B answers "Yes, but..." and comes up with a reason for not doing the activity. (E.g.: A: Let's go for a swim. B: Yes, but I haven't got my swimming trunks.) Next, B makes a counter-suggestion to which A again responds with "Yes, but..." and comes up with yet another reason for not doing the activity.
In the second part of the exercise, A again makes a suggestion. This time, B answers with "Yes, and..." and adds to the activity. A, in turn, responds positively to the addition, and answers with "Yes, and..." and makes an extra suggestion to support the previous suggestions (e.g. A: Shall we go for a swim? B: Yes, and let's also have a go on the water slide. A: Yes, and let's come up with a new swimming stroke.). Ask the participants to also act out the activities — possibly using mime.

Tips & directions
- Demonstrate the exercise to the whole group the first time.
- Be strict about the fact that the pairs have to accept and build on the idea.
- Afterwards, ask the participants how they felt about the different versions? What are the differences in energy? Did they recognize certain situations from their own work environment?

Additional exercise by Patrick Short :

BOBSLED

BOBSLED

Objective explore the dynamics of changing leadership, follow the follower and serving the needs of the team, all while keeping things moving.

Summary moving around the space in teams of four, participants experience volatility, uncertainty, complexity and ambiguity, usually while laughing very hard.

Duration 10-15 minutes, plus reflection time

Number of participants from 4 to 400

Description of the activity

Have the group separate into groups of 4. Each group stands facing one direction, one behind the other, as if they were on a bobsled. People in positions 2, 3 and 4 place their hands on the shoulder of the person in front of them. The leader directs the groups to start moving randomly around the space, without bumping into each other. Start with everyone stepping with their left feet, then their right feet, until they work their way up to walking speed. Once everyone is up to speed, introduce the following commands one at a time (Bobsleds keep moving while all commands are put into action):

Change: The player in front switches to the back of the bobsled.
Rotate: Everyone turns around so the person in the back of the bobsled is now leading, and the person in front is now in back.
Switch: Players 2 and 4 switch positions.
Trade: The third player in each Bobsled changes to third position on *a different Bobsled.*

Once all of the commands are introduced, tell the players that the person who is at the back of the Bobsled will now give the commands.

Adapted from William Hall of BATS.

Alphabetical list of exercises

On the following pages, you can find an alphabetical overview of all exercises. You can also find exercises based on the different chapters to which they are relevant. We've included which exercises are well suited for the start or close of a session in which you use multiple exercises. Furthermore, we proudly present which exercises are the favorite exercises of our ambassadors. Finally, if you want to train a specific habit of the 7 Habits of Great Improvisers, just look at the columns 1-7 for each habit. For easy reference, here are the 7 Habits once more.

Habit 1	Say Yes, And...
Habit 2	Be flexible
Habit 3	Be in moment
Habit 4	Experiment
Habit 5	Use your intuition
Habit 6	Make others look good
Habit 7	Dare to fail

Nr	Name	Chapter	Timing	1	2	3	4	5	6	7	Favorite exercise
1	1 minute		starting			•		•			
2	1-2-3 Clap-Stamp-Scratch	creativity	starting			•			•	•	
3	An alien has landed	multicultural				•	•	•	•	•	
4	Character creation	creativity				•	•				Kat Koppett
5	Circle of emotions				•		•			•	
6	Circle of eye contact					•			•		
7	Circle of sound					•			•		
8	City soundscape		closing				•	•			
9	Clumps	multicultural	starting			•		•	•	•	Alieke van der Wijk
10	Color/Advance				•	•			•	•	
11	Come here, Get outta here	creativity leadership				•		•		•	Henk van der Steen
12	Commitment walk										
13	Count up					•	•	•	•	•	
14	Diamond dance									•	
15	Dolphin training	leadership		•	•	•	•	•			

Nr	Name	Chapter	Timing	1	2	3	4	5	6	7	Favorite exercise
16	Drawing in pairs	creativity leadership			•		•	•		•	
17	Evolution		starting			•			•	•	
18	Experience ring								•		Frans Bosch
19	Exploring status	multicultural					•				
20	Facts and assumptions	multicultural				•		•		•	
21	Faint and support					•			•		
22	Family portraits	creativity			•	•			•		
23	Find the change	creativity					•				
24	Finger applause		closing	•	•		•				
25	Flowerpots	creativity		•	•	•					
26	Free Fall	leadership				•	•				
27	Geographic map	multicultural					•				Nicole van der Ouw
28	Gibberish story	multicultural		•	•		•			•	
29	Greatest Common Denominator		starting		•		•				

Nr	Name	Chapter	Timing	1	2	3	4	5	6	7	Favorite exercise
30	Greeting people		starting		•		•			•	
32	Helping by serving	leadership		•	•		•				
31	Hot spot		starting		•	•			•		
33	Hypeman			•					•		
34	Intelligent clay				•	•	•	•			Belina Raffy
35	Jolly Joseph		starting							•	
36	Leading the blind					•	•	•	•		Renatus Hoogenraad
37	Let's go		closing	•							
38	Letter H	creativity	starting	•	•	•	•		•	•	Bobbi Block
39	Line up		starting		•	•	•			•	
40	Machine		closing	•	•	•	•				
41	Mini-max										
42	Mirror mirror	leadership			•	•			•		Burgert Kirsten
43	One clap		closing					•			
44	One word at a time	creativity			•	•	•			•	
45	Oracle	creativity			•		•			•	

Nr	Name	Chapter	Timing	1	2	3	4	5	6	7	Favorite exercise
46	Orchestra		starting			•		•			
47	Pass the clap		starting			•				•	
48	Pass the patterns				•	•	•			•	Stef Kuypers
49	Pass the zap			•	•		•			•	Viv McWaters
50	Perfect boss			•					•		Matt Weinstein
51	Present					•	•			•	
52	Problem walk	creativity leadership									
53	Psssht		closing			•	•			•	
54	Rain				•	•	•			•	
55	Reverse musical chairs										
56	Rock paper scissors		starting	•					•		
57	Seven strange questions		starting								
58	Shoot-out					•		•	•	•	
59	Shout numbers				•	•	•	•	•	•	Shawn Kinley
60	Snap	creativity			•		•			•	Paul Z Jackson

Nr	Name	Chapter	Timing	1	2	3	4	5	6	7	Favorite exercise
61	Solution walk	creativity leadership		•							
62	Speak as one	creativity			•	•	•		•	•	
63	Statue exhibition	creativity			•		•				
64	Status reception	leadership				•	•				
65	Super president	creativity		•		•	•		•	•	Hikaru Hie
66	Talk in metaphors	multicul-tural		•	•		•				
67	Thought experiment				•	•	•	•			
68	Triangles				•	•	•		•	•	Andre Besseling
69	Walking by numbers	creativity		•	•	•	•		•	•	
70	What are you doing	creativity			•	•	•				
71	What I like about your idea ...	leadership		•							Sue Walden
72	What shape are you in		starting			•		•			Yael Schy
73	Whoosh			•		•	•		•	•	
74	Word association chain			•		•			•	•	
75	Yes but, yes and ...	creativity		•	•	•	•		•		
+1	Bobsled	Customer Service							•		Patrick Short

ABOUT THE AUTHORS

GIJS VAN BILSEN

Gijs van Bilsen is inspiration officer at Pentascope. And that is what he does: inpsire. Inspire people to get up and get moving. Both in a physical asnda symbolic way. He inspires organizations to use more improvisation. To beceome more flexible, innovative and entrepreneurial.

The motivation of Gijs van Bilsen is to help people and organizations to quickly respond to changes in their environment. By teaching people to improvise he lets them see possibilities and quickly solve problems. In this way people learn to cope with a complex and rapidly changing world.

Out of the 7 habits of great improvisers, Yes, Anding and Experimenting describe Gijs best. He loves to initiate new projects and does so with a great amount of positive energy. He believes learning comes from experiencing what does and doesn't work and tries to live accordingly.

Besides this book, Gijs has written a Dutch book on improvisation and communication. He has also published scientific research on organizational improvisation and leadership. Now Yes and… Your Business is finished, Gijs hopes organizations will be inspired to become improvisational organizations and he looks forward to helping them achieve this.

www.pentascope.nl

CYRIEL KORTLEVEN

Cyriel is a much sought-after speaker at conferences, events and internal meetings.

Through his playful and enthusiastic attitude to life, he creates an open and informal atmosphere - ideal for bigger events and conferences. His main subject is creativity and innovation. In a very practical and simple way, he enables the participants to experience the power of creative thinking and doing. His presentations are highly interactive (even when working with big groups) and are always tailored to his audience by using innovative examples from their field. The combination of speaker and creative master of ceremony is also a role Cyriel relishes.

Cyriel is also one of the founders and experts of 21 Lobsterstreet - An energetic bunch of experts, on the job wherever people and organisations are in need for creativity, innovation and change. Working on the edge of intellect and intuition, we take on serious challenges and answer with results.

Cyriel in 21 words:

International speaker, Master of Interaction, 21Lobsterstreet, Knight of NOW, inspirator, author, human being, brainstorm-sessions, large groups, creativity, improvisation, interaction, timespiration, present.

www.cyrielkortleven.com

JOOST KADIJK

As a young child he wanted to be a preacher, impressed by the theatrical magic of the Sunday Masses he attended. He soon discovered the power of theatre and has played several roles in his life. After a study in Health Care Management and Drama, Joost has combined his interest and expertise as trainer, coach and director and author. Together with Cyriel, Joost has written the Dutch version of this book: En...Actie!

After attending several workshops by Keith Johnstone, the founding father of theatrical improvisation, Joost discovered that improv has a lot in common with creativity. You can stimulate creativity through improv and vice-versa. The combination of creativity and improvisation has been a theme in the work of Joost for the last decade.

Joost has worked in the field of innovation and organisational change for over 15 years. His focus is on creating a collaborative, flexible and creative culture. Cultural change is the key element in succesfull organisational development. He has worked as trainer, consultant, project leader and interim manager.

He has initiated several innovation projects in the profit and non-profit sector. He has written books on organisational change and innovation. He likes to share his insights and experiences as facilitator, author, keynote speaker or at the bar. He participates in several ventures developing new solutions for health care, safety and social participation.

Joost is partner of 21, Lobsterstreet

www.21lobsterstreet.com

PATRICK SHORT

Born in Madison, Wisconsin, USA, Patrick has a Bachelor of Arts degree in Biology from Lawrence University and a Master of Fine Arts in Stage Direction from the University of Wisconsin-Madison, where he used improvisation to teach teacher candidates how to integrate theatre arts in the classroom.

Patrick set out for a theatre job in the Bay Area of California and was fired after one year for pestering the boss with too many suggestions for improvement. A temporary job in Customer Service turned into a variety of sales and marketing positions for Altos Computer Systems, which was later purchased by Acer America. Patrick made one suggestion too many to the chairman of Acer America, who threatened to fire him if he ever spoke to him again; Patrick fortunately got a job in sales in Beaverton, Oregon, with one of his best customers, MicroAccounting Systems, Inc. (MASI).

MASI sold manufacturing and distribution systems, and the consultative sales style meant that Patrick got to learn all about how companies worked. And didn't work.

Concurrent with the high-tech career, Patrick began performing and teaching improvisation with ComedySportz-San Jose and, in 1993, founded CSz Portland. In 2000, he left MASI and began managing his business – an improvisational theatre – full time. Since 2002, he has also served as Executive Director of CSz Worldwide, the international organization of ComedySportz producers.

A member of the Applied Improvisation Network, Patrick has guided companies with applied improvisation training since 1989, including Nike, Intel, GE, IBM, Apple and hundreds more. He is also the co-author (with Jill Bernard) of *Jill and Patrick's Small Book of Improv for Business*.

With more than 2500 performances and 1500 workshops taught, Patrick finds time to write and record pop music, coach girl's youth soccer and participate in family life with his wife, Ruth Jenkins (a Speech Pathologist who uses improvisation with her patients and teaches caregivers how to use it), a son, Cowan, and a daughter Fiona. You can reach Patrick through CSz Portland.

www.cszportland.com

About the authors

ACKNOWLEDGEMENTS

Improvising a book while keeping a smile on our face would not have been possible without the help of some very talented people and helpful organizations. First of all, we would like to thank the Applied Improvisation Network (www.appliedimprov.ning.com). This large (2000+ members) and global network does great work in connecting people and helping them spread the power of improvisation. All the people who contributed their favorite exercises are active members of the AIN and they deserve an special mention in. Furthermore, we wish to thank TSM Business School and Twente University for sponsoring the research that underlies chapters 2 and 3.

That leaves us with the most important people, who really sacrificed a lot of time to get this book as beautiful and mistake-free as it is. Philip Chimento gave us his excellent opinion on our English spelling and grammar and Esther Vorstenbosch did an outstanding job with the lay-out. Last but not least, we wish to thank Kathleen Steegmans for designing our website. If you haven't checked out *www.yesandyourbusiness.com*, go to the site right now!

LIST OF AMBASSA-DORS
&
BIBLIO GRAPHY

A special thanks to our ambassadors. These ambassadors contributed to this book and gave their their favorite exercise to use in our toolbox. You can find the list with contact details of all those great people on the next pages.

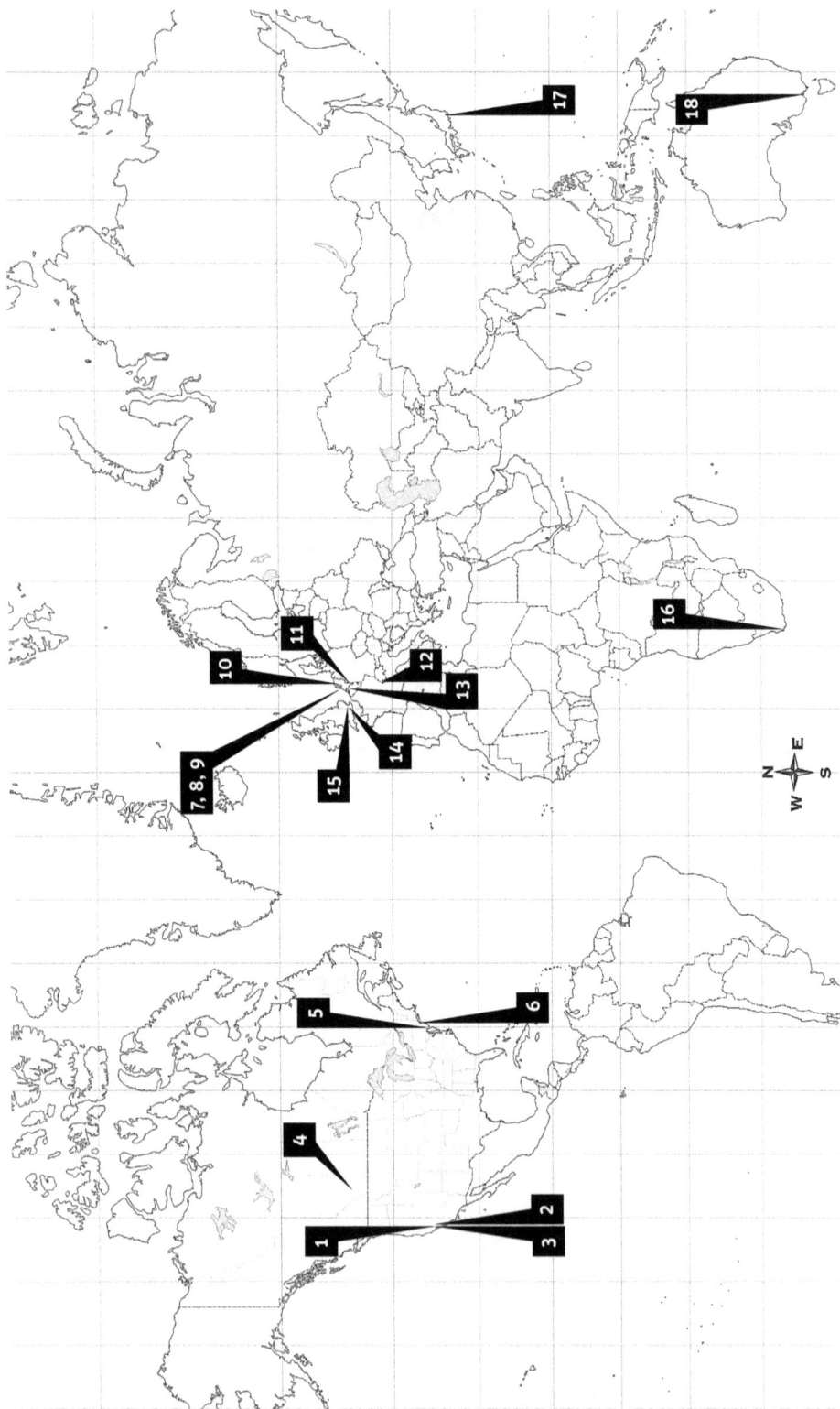

	Name	Location	Favorite exercise
1	Matt Weinstein	Nicasio, CA, USA	Perfect boss
2	Yael Schy	Oakland, CA, USA	What shape are you in
3	Sue Walden	San Francisco, CA, USA	What I like about your idea
4	Shawn Kinley	Traveling the world (based in Calgary, Canada)	Shout numbers
5	Bobbi Block	Philadelphia, PA, USA	Letter H
6	Kat Koppett	New York, NY, USA	Character creation
7	Alieke van der Wijk	Amsterdam, Nederland	Clumps
8	Henk van der Steen	Amsterdam, Nederland	Come here, get outta here
9	Andre Besseling	Amsterdam, Nederland	Triangles
10	Nicole van der Ouw	Ruinen, Nederland	Find the change
11	Frans Bosch	Herkenbosch, Nederland	Experience ring
12	Renatus Hoogenraad	Carouge, Switserland	Leading the blind
13	Stef Kuypers	Antwerpen, België	Pass the patterns
14	Belina Raffy	Esher, UK	Intelligent clay
15	Paul Z Jackson	London, UK	Snap
16	Burgert Kirsten	Stellenbosch, South Africa	Mirror mirror
17	Hikaru Hie	Tokyo, Japan	Super president
18	Viv McWaters	Torquay, Australia	Pass the zap

List of ambassadors

Name Andre Besseling
Organization Improcentrum
Nederland
Email info@andrebesseling.nl
Website www.improcentrum.nl
City Amsterdam - The Netherlands

Name Bobbi Block
Organization Bobbi Block
Email bobbisfblock@gmail.com
Website www.bobbiblock.com
City Philadelphia, PA, USA

Name Frans Bosch
Organization Takkenwerk
Email info@takkenwerk.nu
Website www.takkenwerk.nu
City Herkenbosch -
The Netherlands

Name Hikaru (Lou) Hie
Organization Ena Communication
Inc. / Be Present Club
Email hikaru@ena-comm.com
hikaruhie@gmail.com
Website http://ena-comm.com
City ToKyo – Japan

Name Renatus Hoogenraad
Organization Sparks Training
Email rh@sparks-training.ch
Website www.sparks-training.ch
City Geneva - Switzerland

Name Paul Z Jackson
Organization PJA
Email paul@impro.org.uk
Website www.impro.org.uk
City London - United Kingdom

Name Shawn Kinley
Organization FunAndPlay
& Loose Moose
Email SK@shawnkinley.com
Website Shawnkinley.com and
improworldtour.com
City Calgary, Canada

Name Burgert Kirsten
Organization Playing Mantis
Email burgert@playingmantis.net
Website www.playingmantis.net
City Stellenbosch - South Africa

Name Kat Koppett
Organization Koppett + Company
Email kat@koppett.com
Website www.koppett.com
City New York

Name Stef Kuypers
Organization new shoes today
E-mail stef@newshoestoday.com
Website www.stefkuypers.com
City Antwerp - Belgium

Name Viv McWaters
Organization Beyond the Edge
Email viv@mcwaters.com.au
Website vivmcwaters.com.au
City Melbourne area, Australia

Name Belina Raffy
Organization Maffick Ltd.
Email Belina@maffick.com
Website www.maffick.com
City London - UK

Name Yael Schy
Organization Dramatic Strides
Consulting
Email yael@dramaticstrides.com
Website www.dramaticstrides.com
City Oakland, CA, USA

Name Nicole van der Ouw
Organization
Creatief Verandermanagement
Email nicole@creatiefverander-
management.nl
Website www.creatiefverander-
management.nl
City Ruinen - The Netherlands

Name Henk van der Steen
Organization Troje
Email henk@troje.nl
Website www.troje.nl
City Amsterdam - The Netherlands

Name Alieke van der Wijk
Organization Troje, Improviseren
in de 21e eeuw
Email alieke@troje.nl
Website www.troje.nl
City Amsterdam - The Netherlands

Name Sue Walden
Organization ImprovWorks!
Email sue@improvworks.org
Website www.improvworks.org
City San Francisco - CA – USA

Name Matt Weinstein
Organization Playfair
Email matt@playfair.com
Website www.playfair.com
City Nicasio - CA - USA

Ambassadors and author

Name Patrick Short
Organization CSz Portland
Email patrick@cszportland.com
Website www.cszportland.com
City Portland - OR - USA
Phone +1 503.236.8888

Bibliography

Books

Andre Besseling, *'Theater vanuit het niets'*, 2002, International Theatre & Film Books.

Igor Byttebier, Ramon Vullings, Godelieve Spaas, *'Creativity Today*, 2007, BIS Publishers.

Jim Collins & Jerry Porras, ' *Built to Last: Successful Habits of Visionary Companies'*, 1994, Harper Business.

Robert Greenleaf, '*The servant as leader'*, 1982, Robert K. Greenleaf Center

Charna Halpern ea, '*Truth in comedy'*, 1994, Meriwether Pub.

Christine Hogan, *Facilitating multicultural groups, a practical guide*, 2007, Kogan Page Publishers.

Keith Johnstone, *'Impro'*, 1990, International Theatre & Film Books.

Keith Johnstone, *'Impro for storytellers'*, 1999, Theatre Arts Book.

Joost Kadijk and Cyriel Kortleven, *'En ... Actie!'*, 2007, Thema.

John Kao, *'Jamming: the art and discipline of corporate creativity'*, 1997, Harper Business.

Kat Koppett, *'Training using drama'*, 2002, Kogan Page Limited.

James Kouzes and Barry Posner, *'The Leadership Challenge (4th edition)'*, 2008, Jossey-Bass.

Ben Kuiken, *'De laatste manager'*, 2010, Haystack.

Keith Sawyer, *'Group Genius, the creative power of collaboration'*, 2007, Basic Books.

Articles

Gregg Fraley, *'Shooting an ideation session in the foot'*, 2003, Quirk's Marketing Research.

Adam Lashinsky, *'Larry Page: Google should be like a family'*, 2006, Fortune Magazine, Vol. 154, No. 7, October 2.

Miguel Pina e Cunha, Ken Kamoche & Rita Campos e Cunha, *'Organizational improvisation and leadership: A field study in two computer mediated settings'*, 2003, Int. Studies of Management & Organization, vol, 33, no. 1, Spring 2003, pp, 34-57.